PASSION PLAYS

RANDALL BALMER

PASSION PLAYS

How Religion Shaped Sports in North America

FF

A FERRIS AND FERRIS BOOK

The University of North Carolina Press
CHAPEL HILL

This book was published under the Marcie Cohen Ferris and William R. Ferris Imprint of the University of North Carolina Press.

© 2022 Randall Balmer

All rights reserved
Set in Scala Pro, Avenir LT Std & Museo Slab
by codeMantra
Manufactured in the United States of America

The University of North Carolina Press has been a member of the Green Press Initiative since 2003.

Cover photo © iStockphoto/NiseriN.

Complete Library of Congress Cataloging-in-Publication Data is available at https://lccn.loc.gov/2022015059.

ISBN 978-1-4696-7006-5 (cloth: alk. paper)
ISBN 978-1-4696-7007-2 (ebook)

FOR MARY AND JOHN MURRIN

To every thing there is a season, and a time to
every purpose under the heaven.

—Ecclesiastes 3:1

A ballpark at night is more like a church than a church.

—W. P. Kinsella

Any object, intensely regarded, may be a gate of
access to the incorruptible eon of the gods.

—James Joyce

CONTENTS

ILLUSTRATIONS

PASSION PLAYS

To Everything a Season

The Peculiar Passion Surrounding
Team Sports

Similarly, if anyone competes as an athlete, he does not receive the
victor's crown unless he competes according to the rules.

—2 TIMOTHY 2:5

Play is the forerunner of religion, so religion
should be the friend of play.

—HORACE BUSHNELL

The immediate catalyst for this book was my discovery of sports radio
sometime in the early 1990s. Initially, it left me speechless. I was utterly
dumbfounded that radio hosts could sustain a conversation and a debate
for hours and hours about whether or not Joe Torre—I was working
in New York City at the time—should have pulled the starting pitcher
with two outs in the bottom of the sixth, or whether the Jets should have
punted on fourth-and-one at the forty-three-yard line. What entranced me
was the passion that both hosts and callers brought to the subject. Vinny
from Queens worried about the back end of the Yankees' starting rota-
tion, Doris from Rego Park regularly fretted over the Mets' bullpen, and
Jerome from Manhattan worked himself into a lather over the composition of the Yankees' roster, becoming so apoplectic in the course of his
calls that his physician finally ordered him to stop calling. The rhetoric

grew so fevered you might think the topic was nuclear disarmament or the collapse of democratic institutions, not whether the Twins should have used Joe Mauer as a pinch-hitter in the top of the eighth inning.[1]

To take another example, in early 2015 the world of sports—and much of the nation—was abuzz about allegations that the New England Patriots had tampered with the footballs used in their playoff victory over the Indianapolis Colts. For me, the more interesting question is why we care so much about matters such as these. In a world wracked by war and disease and terrorism and political upheaval, why was so much ink spilled over whether or not a couple of pounds of air pressure mysteriously went missing from a dozen or so footballs? Why do we care so much about whether Tom Brady was slinging underinflated footballs into the night sky? It's only a game, right?

I've enjoyed sports all my life, both as participant and spectator, and I have my team allegiances, but I would never describe myself as a hard-core or, to employ the vernacular of sports radio, "die-hard" or "big-time" fan. But the longer I listened—and I confess that I became addicted—the more I wanted to figure out why sports invokes such peculiar passion. That is the burden of this book, and in a very real sense it represents an attempt to understand myself.

Passion Plays examines how the history of religion across North America connects in fascinating ways to the emergence of modern team sports—and this chronicle in turn illustrates why sports inspires such passionate intensity. *Passion Plays* argues that sports has evolved into a phenomenon that generates at least as much passion as traditional religion. Drawing on indices of popularity and devotion, I will suggest that, especially among the demographic of white males, the devotion to sports has eclipsed allegiance to traditional expressions of religion. To be clear, I am not arguing that sports is a religion in any conventional sense of the word, even though there are family resemblances between the two. Team sports may provide a sense of community, perhaps, or take on some of the trappings of religion—processions, sacred space, pilgrimage—but sports does not forgive sins or grant salvation. The world of sports provides many narratives of redemption, both individual and collective—a woeful team's ascent from worst to first, Kurt Warner's rise from supermarket stock boy to Super Bowl–winning quarterback and the Hall of

Fame, David Ayres's summons from the Zamboni to serve as emergency goalie and notch a win for the Carolina Hurricanes, Sean Kazmar's promotion to the major leagues at the age of thirty-four. But such stories, inspiring as they are, don't carry the cosmic weight of a Lakota sun dance or the burning of Zozobra in New Mexico, Hindu purification rituals, or the drama of redemption described in the New Testament. Sports can teach us about the physics of speed or the economics of the salary cap or the vagaries of the infield fly rule, but it provides precious little help deciphering the mysteries of the universe. Nevertheless, as even a cursory glance at the stands will attest, there are undeniable parallels between (sports) fans and (religious) fanatics, and it is at least arguable that the real locus of popular devotion in North America has shifted from the sanctuary to the stadium.[2]

Not all sports fans, it must be acknowledged, gravitated to the stadium directly from church. Many were long accustomed to finding more meaning, depth, profundity, ultimacy, community, and even salvation on any given Saturday at the ballpark than at last Sunday's mass. For them, sports has always been at least as important as religion, perhaps more so.

Competitive team sports developed in North America at a time of rapid social, economic, political, demographic—and religious—change. From the emergence of baseball in the 1840s to the invention of basketball in 1891, North America was in transition. The Industrial Revolution created vast disparities of wealth, but it also altered patterns of subsistence and male sociability; men began working outside of the farms and socialized with fellow workers. Americans gravitated toward the cities, where they encountered immigrants from Ireland, Germany, Italy, Scandinavia, and other places. Railroad lines knitted the continent together in something resembling a tapestry, making frontiers accessible. Canadians were forging their national identity at the same time the United States played out its moral crisis on the battlefields of Bull Run, Gettysburg, Antietam, and Chickamauga, exacting a fearsome toll of casualties, roughly 2 percent of the nation's population.

The evolution of the four major team sports in North America—baseball, football, hockey, and basketball—coincided with these social changes, and in some ways they are intimately related. The development of the telegraph and the railroad, for instance, made both intercollegiate and professional leagues possible, allowing the travel of teams from one community to another and news about the contests to filter back to hometowns. The move from subsistence living to factories provided at least the possibility of discretionary income and leisure time, and thereby a pool of both players and spectators.

The sports themselves reflected these changes. The violence of football, played by the sons, nephews, and brothers of Union army officers at elite Northeastern schools, recalled the carnage of Civil War battlefields, while baseball reflected the immigrant experience, even as it pushed against the constraints of industrialization. The Canadian embrace of lacrosse and then hockey coincided with emerging Canadian nationalism, and it derived from an intentional break with English traditions in favor of a rough game that evoked the brutality and the frontier justice of Canada's vast expanses of wilderness. Basketball, an urban game, mimicked the complexities of life in the city precisely at the moment when cities were burgeoning.

Each sport, therefore, reflected, or reacted against, the zeitgeist: baseball and the Industrial Revolution, football and the Civil War, hockey and the formation of the Canadian Confederation, basketball and urbanization. Each sport in turn developed certain characteristics and meanings that help to explain its appeal in different eras, in different regions, and to different demographic groups.

The social changes of the nineteenth century also created anxieties. The Victorian-era cult of domesticity made white, middle-class women sovereigns of their households and the moral guardians of both their families and society. At least since the late seventeenth century (the earliest data we have), women have dominated religious life in North America while men's participation lagged. With the advent of the Industrial Revolution in the nineteenth century, many husbands no longer worked the land, passing their days instead at the factory or in some sedentary office job, with little access to fresh air and few opportunities for exercise.

Several remedies were proposed, including camping and fraternal organizations. The nineteenth-century movement that became known as Muscular Christianity originated in the British novels of Thomas Hughes and Charles Kingsley, which valorized robust, athletic Christians. Awash in fears that Anglicans had succumbed to effeminacy, various church-men began advocating for rigorous physical exercise as an antidote to the enervating effects of urban life during the Industrial Revolution. Muscu-lar Christianity crossed the Atlantic and was picked up by a diverse array of proponents, all of them apologists for a strenuous religion.[3]

In North America, the Muscular Christianity movement was adopted by Protestant churchmen in the decades following the Civil War, and it included such initiatives and innovations as the Young Men's Christian Association (YMCA), church-league athletics, the Men and Religion For-ward movement of the 1910s, and most recently, Promise Keepers. Draw-ing on the New Testament metaphors of militarism ("the full armor of God") and athleticism ("running the race," "finishing the course"), Prot-estant leaders jettisoned the Puritan aversion to sports as frivolity and recommended a strenuous life marked by athletic pursuits and aggres-sive, even pugilistic, male behavior. Therein lay an antidote to overly fem-inized churches as well as the revival of "old stock" Protestantism against the incursion of non-Protestant immigrants.

Muscular Christianity, then, served both religious and sociological ends. In the early decades of the twentieth century, large churches incor-porated basketball courts and bowling alleys into their physical plants in what became known as the institutional church movement. Roman Catholics followed suit. The Catholic Youth Organization (CYO), with its boxing tournaments and basketball games, was begun in Chicago in 1930 and spread across North America and the world; Catholic athletic leagues fostered competition among schools and gave rise to pep ban-ners bearing such memorable sentiments as BEAT HOLY CHILD. Juda-ism emulated the YMCA with Young Men's Hebrew Associations, and Reconstructionist Judaism sought to mimic institutional churches.[4]

Many of the leaders of organized team sports were connected in some way or another with Muscular Christianity, and all of the sports them-selves emerged out of a specific historical and cultural context. But, as with the unpredictability of the games themselves, the world of sports often confounded the intentions and the aspirations of its founders while simultaneously functioning as an engine for social change, especially on matters of race and ethnicity.

In the second half of the nineteenth century, the four major team sports in North America—baseball, football, hockey, and basketball—were devised in the Northeast and can be plotted in a geographical arc from Princeton and New Brunswick, New Jersey, to New York City to New Haven, Connecticut, and Springfield, Massachusetts, to Montréal. Other formative developments occurred not far away from that arc: the first known reference to baseball in Pittsfield, Massachusetts, the first rugby-style football game in Cambridge, Massachusetts, and the first international hockey game in Burlington, Vermont.

After examining the beginnings, evolution, and symbolism of each sport, I will suggest that the increased passion for sports in recent decades has, for many, displaced traditional expressions of religion. Connections between body and spirit have been drawn since at least the classical period, which generated an impetus for physical exertion and athletic competition. Ancient Greeks believed that the development of mind, body, and spirit were linked, that physical training produced both endurance and patience, and that athletic triumph represented a credit to both athletic and moral virtues. Just as Aristotle's *Nicomachean Ethics* posited that moral virtues could be cultivated and strengthened, so too physical attributes could be enhanced through training. A Greek gymnasium provided facilities for athletic training and competition as well as a place for discussing philosophy, religion, music, and current events.

The absence of a distinction between mind and body in the classical world has resonance today. Drawing on both science and spirituality, many elite athletes now pay attention to the mind-body continuum in their training regimens and game preparations.

The parallels between sports and religion—sacred space, ritual, authoritative texts—underscore the affinities between the two. The specter of National Hockey League champions drinking champagne from the Stanley Cup, for example, is surely reminiscent of the Holy Eucharist, no less than the penalty box resembles a confessional. The Baseball Hall of Fame, Frank Deford writes, "closely approximates a Catholic shrine." Like religion, the world of sports provides the oasis of an orderly universe, precisely because the world around us is not fair or rational or unambiguous—or orderly. For a couple of hours on a lazy summer

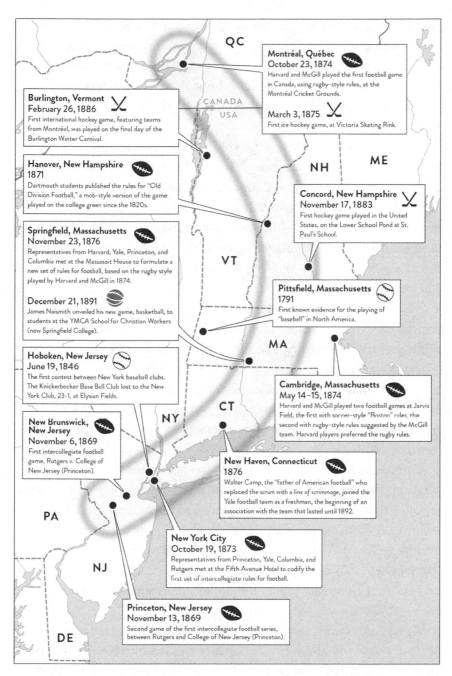

Montréal, Québec
October 23, 1874
Harvard and McGill played the first football game in Canada, using rugby-style rules, at the Montréal Cricket Grounds.

March 3, 1875
First ice hockey game, at Victoria Skating Rink.

Burlington, Vermont
February 26, 1886
First international hockey game, featuring teams from Montréal, was played on the final day of the Burlington Winter Carnival.

Hanover, New Hampshire
1871
Dartmouth students published the rules for "Old Division Football," a mob-style version of the game played on the college green since the 1820s.

Concord, New Hampshire
November 17, 1883
First hockey game played in the United States, on the Lower School Pond at St. Paul's School.

Springfield, Massachusetts
November 23, 1876
Representatives from Harvard, Yale, Princeton, and Columbia met at the Massasoit House to formulate a new set of rules for football, based on the rugby style played by Harvard and McGill in 1874.

December 21, 1891
James Naismith unveiled his new game, basketball, to students at the YMCA School for Christian Workers (now Springfield College).

Pittsfield, Massachusetts
1791
First known evidence for the playing of "baseball" in North America.

Hoboken, New Jersey
June 19, 1846
The first contest between New York baseball clubs. The Knickerbocker Base Ball Club lost to the New York Club, 23-1, at Elysian Fields.

Cambridge, Massachusetts
May 14–15, 1874
Harvard and McGill played two football games at Jarvis Field, the first with soccer-style "Boston" rules, the second with rugby-style rules suggested by the McGill team. Harvard players preferred the rugby rules.

New Brunswick, New Jersey
November 6, 1869
First intercollegiate football game, Rutgers v. College of New Jersey (Princeton).

New Haven, Connecticut
1876
Walter Camp, the "father of American football" who replaced the scrum with a *line of scrimmage*, joined the Yale football team as a freshman, the beginning of an association with the team that lasted until 1892.

New York City
October 19, 1873
Representatives from Princeton, Yale, Columbia, and Rutgers met at the Fifth Avenue Hotel to codify the first set of intercollegiate rules for football.

Princeton, New Jersey
November 13, 1869
Second game of the first intercollegiate football series, between Rutgers and College of New Jersey (Princeton).

QC · CANADA · USA · NH · ME · VT · MA · CT · NY · PA · NJ · DE

The invention and development of major team sports in North America occurred on a geographical arc from Princeton, New Jersey, to Montréal, Québec. Other formative events—in Springfield and Cambridge, Massachusetts, and Burlington, Vermont—took place not far outside of that arc. Erin Greb Cartography.

afternoon or three or four hours on Super Bowl Sunday, we can all retreat into at least the illusion of a world of clarity, what appears to be a near-perfect meritocracy where every contestant competes on an equal footing, where the receiver did or did not make the catch before falling out of bounds, and where a winner will be declared at game's end. It's a wonderful and enchanted world.[5]

Even the geometricality of the sports field itself reinforces the quest for order. "Nothing is more orderly and geometrically precise than baseball," according to A. Bartlett Giamatti. The playing fields of football, soccer, and basketball are defined by right angles, and both of the partial exceptions to this pattern—the baseball outfield and a hockey rink—have their share of angles. Geometry prevails in organized sports, which reinforces a sense of order. And what do we say when a team is victorious? They won fair and square.[6]

In addition, sports provides perhaps the closest approximation of a meritocracy that we have—even though it is undeniable that, because of race, gender, or privilege, access to the arena is easier for some than others. At least at the higher competitive levels, however, unless you are talented at whatever game you choose, you will not succeed, and you may even be denied the opportunity to compete. Sports, for all its blemishes, may come closer to the ideal of democracy than any other institution in American culture.

Although I'm intrigued by the parallels between religion and sport—stadiums as sacred space, game-day ritual and liturgy, and so on—I want to argue that Americans have a deeper, visceral connection with sports, in terms of both its popularity and the devotion of its adherents. This affinity derives in part from the nature of the games themselves as well as from the religious history that I will trace alongside other cultural, social, and political circumstances in the decades surrounding the turn of the twenty-first century.

I make no claims here for American exceptionalism; people in other parts of the world are, I'm sure, equally passionate about sports, especially the game they call *football*, what Americans refer to as soccer, as is evident whenever the World Cup is contested. But as an American historian, and specifically a historian of religion in North America, it strikes me as worthy of comment that a society once distinguished for its religiosity—belief in God, religious adherence—has become a hothouse for sports.

What follows represents my attempt to understand why.

In *Passion Plays*, I focus on the formative moments and circumstances that suggest the larger context, meaning, and symbolism of each of the four major team sports. General and comprehensive histories of sports in North America abound elsewhere, and I also want to move beyond a survey of "bivocational" athletes, figures like Billy Sunday, outfielder for the Chicago White Stockings who became a famous evangelist; Reggie "the Minister of Defense" White, who was both an evangelical pastor and a fearsome defensive end; or Tim Tebow, Heisman Trophy winner, sometime NFL quarterback, and unabashed Christian. My purpose is to demonstrate that we cannot completely understand why sports invokes such peculiar passion unless we delve into the history and symbolism of team sports and their relationship to organized religion and to the broader historical context. Indeed, the history and the evolution of team sports in North America are braided with religious institutions (YMCAs, church leagues, the University of Notre Dame) and individuals with explicit religious commitments (Anthony Bowen, John Franklin Crowell, James Naismith, Amos Alonzo Stagg, Hank Greenberg, Branch Rickey). Jewish sportswriters both prodded and applauded the desegregation of professional sports. Because of this intersection between religion and team sports from their very beginnings, it is no small irony that, for many Americans, these sports have displaced traditional expressions of religion; especially among the demographic of white males, attention to sports has increasingly eclipsed religious devotion.

Although I acknowledge the arguments for including other sports— soccer, for instance—I've restricted my focus to baseball, football, hockey, and basketball. These seem to me the most popular in North America, especially at the collegiate and professional levels, but I find especially compelling the historical contexts for their emergence as well as the religious influences that helped to shape them. For that reason, I have focused on the history of these sports during their formative decades, roughly from the mid-nineteenth to the mid-twentieth centuries, by which time the conventions surrounding each sport had taken their

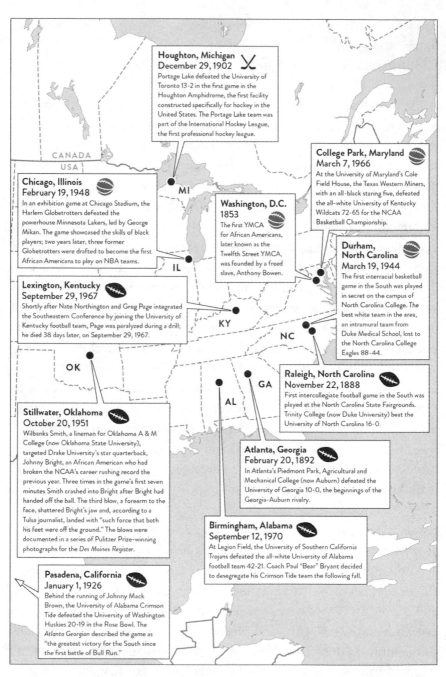

Houghton, Michigan
December 29, 1902
Portage Lake defeated the University of Toronto 13-2 in the first game in the Houghton Amphidrome, the first facility constructed specifically for hockey in the United States. The Portage Lake team was part of the International Hockey League, the first professional hockey league.

College Park, Maryland
March 7, 1966
At the University of Maryland's Cole Field House, the Texas Western Miners, with an all-black staring five, defeated the all-white University of Kentucky Wildcats 72-65 for the NCAA Basketball Championship.

Chicago, Illinois
February 19, 1948
In an exhibition game at Chicago Stadium, the Harlem Globetrotters defeated the powerhouse Minnesota Lakers, led by George Mikan. The game showcased the skills of black players; two years later, three former Globetrotters were drafted to become the first African Americans to play on NBA teams.

Washington, D.C.
1853
The first YMCA for African Americans, later known as the Twelfth Street YMCA, was founded by a freed slave, Anthony Bowen.

Durham, North Carolina
March 19, 1944
The first interracial basketball game in the South was played in secret on the campus of North Carolina College. The best white team in the area, an intramural team from Duke Medical School, lost to the North Carolina College Eagles 88-44.

Lexington, Kentucky
September 29, 1967
Shortly after Nate Northington and Greg Page integrated the Southeastern Conference by joining the University of Kentucky football team, Page was paralyzed during a drill; he died 38 days later, on September 29, 1967.

Raleigh, North Carolina
November 22, 1888
First intercollegiate football game in the South was played at the North Carolina State Fairgrounds. Trinity College (now Duke University) beat the University of North Carolina 16-0.

Stillwater, Oklahoma
October 20, 1951
Wilbanks Smith, a lineman for Oklahoma A & M College (now Oklahoma State University), targeted Drake University's star quarterback, Johnny Bright, an African American who had broken the NCAA's career rushing record the previous year. Three times in the game's first seven minutes Smith crashed into Bright after Bright had handed off the ball. The third blow, a forearm to the face, shattered Bright's jaw and, according to a Tulsa journalist, landed with "such force that both his feet were off the ground." The blows were documented in a series of Pulitzer Prize-winning photographs for the *Des Moines Register*.

Atlanta, Georgia
February 20, 1892
In Atlanta's Piedmont Park, Agricultural and Mechanical College (now Auburn) defeated the University of Georgia 10-0, the beginnings of the Georgia-Auburn rivalry.

Birmingham, Alabama
September 12, 1970
At Legion Field, the University of Southern California Trojans defeated the all-white University of Alabama football team 42-21. Coach Paul "Bear" Bryant decided to desegregate his Crimson Tide team the following fall.

Pasadena, California
January 1, 1926
Behind the running of Johnny Mack Brown, the University of Alabama Crimson Tide defeated the University of Washington Huskies 20-19 in the Rose Bowl. The *Atlanta Georgian* described the game as "the greatest victory for the South since the first battle of Bull Run."

Notable developments in team sports outside of New England. Erin Greb Cartography.

current form. I'm well aware of the challenges facing each of the major sports in the twenty-first century—the languid pace of baseball games in an internet age, the concussions and violence of football, the inability of even middle-class parents to afford the expenses of junior hockey—but this is not a book that presumes to offer prescriptions for the survival and perpetuation of each of these sports, let alone sports in general.[7]

Finally, the crucial matters of race, ethnicity, gender, and sexuality inevitably find their way into this narrative in unexpected ways, and sometimes in ways that should trouble everyone. Black teams and leagues emerged at roughly the same time as white teams, for example, albeit on parallel tracks. These entities, which one historian has called "sporting congregations," had their own integrity and culture; they were not simply waiting passively for integration. Without pretending that women have attained legal, social, or economic parity with men, it is also true that most twenty-first-century institutions, in theory at least, aspire not to discriminate on the basis of sex. Team sports, by and large, are an exception, although transgender athletes are challenging even that. Despite the vastly increased participation of women in organized athletics in recent years, team sports remains an overwhelmingly masculinized, even hypermasculinized, domain, a place where men—both participants and fans—allow themselves to express a range of emotions. It is also a domain where many women feel excluded, even as fans. The racial desegregation of organized sports by the middle of the twentieth century, to take another example, set up the paradox of white fans cheering for athletes of color, even as many fans resent players for expressing themselves, especially their political views, off the field. Part of my argument is that team sports in North America appeals disproportionately to men, especially white men, who find in sports an alternative, orderly universe very much in contrast to their perceptions of an unfair, chaotic world all around them. For them, sports supplies a kind of refuge, one not unlike the one that their faith once provided.[8]

A careful examination of the history of religion and the emergence of team sports in North America reveals all sorts of interconnections, beginning with the mythology surrounding the origins of baseball.

CHAPTER 1

It Breaks Your Heart

The Industrial Revolution and
the Origins of Baseball

Man may penetrate the outer reaches of the universe, he
may solve the very secret to eternity itself, but for me,
the ultimate human experience is to witness the
flawless execution of the hit-and-run.

—BRANCH RICKEY

It's not a sport, it's a religion. It takes on new beliefs
with the greatest of reluctance.

—JIM MURRAY

The mythical origins of baseball are, literally, too good to be true. On a
warm summer morning, June 12, 1839, Abner Doubleday devised the
game of baseball in front of Cooper's Tailor Shop in Cooperstown, New
York. The game was an improvement over an earlier iteration called town
ball, and Doubleday's new version was played nearby in Elihu Phinney's
cow pasture, between students at Otsego Academy and Green's Select
School. Like Jesus tracing letters in the sand in St. John's Gospel, Doubleday first sketched the player positions in the dirt with a stick and later
drew them on a piece of paper together with rudimentary rules of the
game.[1]

It's a wonderful story, one that has insinuated itself into American
folklore. It emphasizes the pastoral nature of the game—played on a

Abner Doubleday (1819–1893), Union Army
general in the Civil War, who did *not* invent the
game of baseball. National Baseball Hall of
Fame and Museum, Cooperstown, N.Y.

grassy field during the idyllic days of summer in a relatively remote loca-
tion hard by Otsego Lake, between the Adirondacks and the Catskills in
central New York. So compelling was this origins narrative that when
Stephen Clark, a Cooperstown philanthropist, asked Ford C. Frick, president of the National League, if he would support a baseball Hall of Fame
in Cooperstown, Frick readily agreed. The inaugural class—Ty Cobb,
Christy Mathewson, Honus Wagner, Walter Johnson, and Babe Ruth—
was inducted on June 12, 1939, in a gala ceremony timed to coincide with
the supposed centennial of baseball. A throng of fans gathered for the
induction and for the dedication of the building emblazoned with COO-
PERSTOWN: BIRTHPLACE OF BASEBALL.[2]

Abner Doubleday, of course, the putative creator of the game, was
not present for the ceremonies on the centennial of his invention. Doubleday, a two-star general for the Union army during the Civil War, had
died in Mendham, New Jersey, in 1893 and was laid to rest in Arlington

National Cemetery. He had lived an eventful life, not only as the officer who fired the first shots in defense of Fort Sumter, but also as commander of Union troops at the Second Battle of Bull Run (Manassas), the Battle of Antietam, and the Battle of Gettysburg. Following the war, while stationed in San Francisco, Doubleday secured a patent for the city's cable-car system. Upon his return to the East Coast, he served as president of the Theosophical Society.

Although Doubleday was not able to attend the centennial celebration in Cooperstown, he was not forgotten. Cribbing shamelessly from Abraham Lincoln's Gettysburg Address, *Time* magazine reported, "The world will little note nor long remember what [Doubleday] did at Gettysburg, but it can never forget what he did at Cooperstown."[3]

Doubleday was not present in Cooperstown for the centennial; neither, it turns out, had he been in Cooperstown the day he purportedly invented baseball. He was a twenty-year-old cadet at West Point. Doubleday, a bookish sort with little appetite for sports, never in the course of his seventy-three years claimed credit for inventing the game of baseball.[4]

The origins of the Doubleday myth, however, reveal a great deal about the nature of baseball itself. Albert Goodwill Spalding, former pitcher and president of the Chicago White Stockings, was eager to establish that baseball was an American invention and not a British import, a derivation of rounders or cricket. In 1888, Spalding had accompanied a group of star players on a world tour to promote the game of baseball, an itinerary that included a game adjacent to the Great Pyramids of Egypt. Upon their return to the United States, Spalding and the players attended a celebratory dinner at Delmonico's, New York City's most exclusive restaurant, an event that drew such luminaries as Mark Twain and Theodore Roosevelt. In the course of the proceedings, Twain offered a paean to baseball, "the very symbol, the outward and visible expression, of the drive and push and rush and struggle of the living, tearing, booming nineteenth, the mightiest of all centuries!"[5]

One of the themes of the evening was baseball's role as America's ambassador to the world as well as its indigenous origins. Abraham Gilbert Mills, the evening's emcee who had been the fourth president of the National League, declared that baseball was "American in its origin" and "in its present perfected state, an evolution of American genius." The festivities were punctuated by occasional chants of "No rounders! No rounders!"[6]

Spalding's quest to vindicate baseball's American origins assumed new urgency early in the twentieth century. Henry Chadwick, sometimes called the "father of baseball" for his early reporting on the game and for his invention of the box score, had written an article in 1903 positing that baseball had descended from the English games of cricket and rounders. Spalding, a pitcher from 1871 to 1878 and, with his brother, cofounder of a sporting goods store in Chicago that evolved into an empire, set out to refute Chadwick's claims. Baseball, Spalding asserted, was a thoroughly American invention. "Our good old American game of baseball must have an American Dad," Spalding wrote to Tim Murnane, sportswriter for the *Boston Globe*. In a letter to another Bostonian, John Lowell, Spalding solicited help because he was "trying to convince myself and others that the American game of Base Ball is purely of American origin, and I want to get all the facts I can to support that theory." Spalding acknowledged that he was motivated by patriotism.[7]

In 1905, the Special Base Ball Commission was charged with discovering the true origins of the game. Better known as the Mills Commission, headed by A. G. Mills, the former president of the National League (and emcee at the New York City celebration), the commission sent out a general appeal for anyone to contribute information germane to the earliest days of baseball.

The notice, published among other places in the *Akron Beacon Journal*, caught the eye of Abner C. Graves, a mining engineer from Denver traveling through town and staying at the Hotel Thuma. Graves responded to the paper with his Doubleday-Cooperstown narrative, which the *Beacon Journal* promptly published. (Graves himself was only five years old when he supposedly witnessed the invention of baseball.) Doubleday's most important innovation, Graves said, was to decrease the number of players on the field to eleven on a side, thereby limiting the incidence of collisions. Spalding sent a follow-up letter to Graves, dated November 10, 1905, asking for more details and seeking sources who might corroborate the story. Graves, who spent time in mental asylums, responded by vacillating on the year—he said it was either 1839, 1840, or 1841—and

Abraham Gilbert Mills (1844–1929), the fourth
president of the National League, headed the
Mills Commission, which concluded that baseball
was invented in Cooperstown, New York.
New York Public Library.

acknowledging that Doubleday's sketch of the ball field and the position-
ing of players had not survived.[8]

As the end of the Mills Commission mandate approached, Mills read
the assembled materials and summarized his findings on December 30,
1907. "I cannot say that I find myself in accord with those who urge the
American origin of the game as against its English origin," Mills wrote.
But the letter then serpentines through ancient Greece, the Chaldean
Empire, and the invention of electricity toward its improbable, italicized
conclusion: *"First: That 'Base Ball' had its origins in the United States. Second: That the first scheme for playing it, according to the best evidence obtain-
able to date, was devised by Abner Doubleday at Cooperstown, N.Y., in 1839."*[9]

Members of the Mills Commission unanimously concurred with the
chair's conclusions, and *Spalding's Guide* triumphantly published the
findings. Henry Chadwick, the titular editor of the guide, wrote to Mills

on the day of publication and congratulated him on "a masterly piece of special pleading." He characterized his disputation with Spalding over the origins of baseball as "a Joke between Albert and myself, for the fun of the thing," but he also noted that the Philadelphia Town Ball Club had played under the rounders rules in 1831, eight years prior to Doubleday's putative invention.[10]

The real origins of baseball are rather more prosaic. Historians have noted the similarity to the English bat-and-ball games of cricket, old cat, and rounders—and to the Dutch game called stool ball. The British publisher John Newbery came out with what is generally regarded as the first children's book, *A Little Pretty Pocket Book*, a volume of rhymes corresponding to letters of the alphabet. It includes the following:

BASE-BALL.
The Ball once struck off,
Away flies the Boy
To the next destin'd Post,
And then Home with Joy.

A Little Pretty Pocket Book appeared in Britain in 1744 and was published in colonial America in 1762.[11]

In 1791, the town council of Pittsfield, Massachusetts, responding to complaints about broken windows, passed a bylaw prohibiting anyone from playing "baseball" within eighty yards of the town's new meetinghouse. The statute mentioned "Wicket, Cricket, Baseball, Batball, Football, Cats, Fives or any other Game or Games with Balls," thereby providing evidence that baseball was a distinct game. Violators faced a fine of five shillings.[12]

The decades from 1791 until the Civil War are littered with cryptic references to "ball," "town ball," "round ball," and "base ball" in places like Philadelphia and Erie, Pennsylvania; New Bedford and Cambridge, Massachusetts; Belfast, Portland, and Waterville, Maine; Beachville, Ontario; Portsmouth and Hanover, New Hampshire; Milwaukee; Troy, Michigan; Buffalo and Rochester, New York; and places as far flung as St. John, New Brunswick; New Orleans; and Honolulu, Hawai'i. Members of the New

Harmony commune in Indiana, founded by Robert Owen, played ball. Students at Exeter, Brown, Yale, Columbia, Georgetown, Hobart, Middlebury, and the University of Michigan enjoyed the game. Blacks and whites played ball together in Harvard Yard. Henry Wadsworth Longfellow, then a student at Bowdoin College, noted in 1824 "that there is nothing now heard of, in our leisure hours, but ball, ball, ball." Organized baseball came to Princeton in the fall of 1858, prompted by the arrival of first-year students from Brooklyn, where the game was more common. The following year, at a neutral site in Pittsfield, Massachusetts, Amherst College defeated Williams 73–32 in twenty-six innings, the first ever intercollegiate baseball game. The first recorded baseball game in Victoria, British Columbia, was played in March 1863.[13]

Many people, including the authorities in some of these venues, clearly regarded ball-playing as a nuisance, echoing the earlier concerns in Pittsfield. Some of the objections were motivated by Sabbatarian scruples. "Is this a Christian country?" a letter to the *New York Evening Post* asked in 1801. "Are there no laws, human or divine, to enforce the religious observance of the Sabbath?" In 1815, students in a religious society at Dartmouth College debated the propriety of "joining in the common amusement of ballplaying." Legislation in Indianapolis in 1837 mandated the fine of one dollar for anyone "who shall on the Sabbath day play at cricket, bandy, cat, town ball, corner ball, or any other game of ball within the limits of the corporation."[14]

Other municipalities, like Providence, Rhode Island; Norwich, Connecticut; or Baltimore, simply wanted to maintain a measure of order. On March 4, 1845, for example, the city of Cleveland acted to mitigate the destructive effects of playing ball in public spaces. Although earlier legislation had outlawed baseball in the public square, "the public was not easily dissuaded from playing." The new ordinance declared that "it should be unlawful for any person or persons to play at any game of Ball, or at any other game or pastime whereby the grass or grounds of any Public place or square shall be defaced or injured." The ban was lifted the following year.[15]

Baseball emerged at a time when some observers worried that, with the advent of the Industrial Revolution, American men were falling behind their English counterparts in "manliness" and athletic development. A letter to the *New York Daily Times* in 1856 refuted that notion, commending the salubrious effects of baseball, a game "that requires strong bones, tough muscle and sound mind; and no athletic game is better calculated to strengthen the frame and develop a full, broad chest, testing a man's powers of endurance most severely." The letter noted that the ball fields of Brooklyn, Harlem, Jersey City, and Hoboken were filled with "youths, who, after working at the desk the greater part of the day in hard mental labor are here developing their physical force, and building up for themselves a constitution anything but 'feeble and enervated.'"[16]

The poet Walt Whitman addressed the same issue, albeit in more elegiac language. He worried that men in nearly every American city were deficient in exercise, that clerks and apprentices toiled long hours in fetid offices and either went home to bed or squandered their free time in less edifying venues. He lamented that "all classes seem to act as though there were no commendable objects of pursuit in the world except making money and tenaciously sticking to one's trade or occupation." Baseball, Whitman believed, provided an antidote. "In our sun-down perambulations of late through the outer parts of Brooklyn, we have observed several parties of youngsters playing 'base,' a certain game of ball," the poet wrote in 1846. "The game of ball is glorious," he continued. "I see great things in baseball. It is our game, the American game. Baseball will take people out of doors, fill them with oxygen, give them a larger physical stoicism, tend to relieve us from being a nervous, dyspeptic set, repair those losses and be a blessing to us."[17]

In addition to its general health benefits, baseball appealed to weary industrial workers, offering a respite from the tedium and drudgery of the factory or the office; it was especially prevalent among those in the printing trades. A popular song that appeared in 1857, "The Baseball Fever," captured the mood:

Our merchants have to close their stores
Their clerks away are staying,
Contractors too, can do no work,
Their hands are all out playing.

Charles King Newcomb, a baseball fan in Philadelphia, understood the appeal to laborers. They "leave the shade & quiet of a shop for the sun &

fury of a ball-ground; they stand & they exercise, for hours, at a strict & laborious game; they attest that they mean to be men & not machines."[18]

The sense of play was essential to the popularity of baseball. Players and teams certainly were competitive, but a spirit of camaraderie prevailed as the teams frequently retired to a tavern after the game. Newcomb, the Philadelphia spectator, a Brown University alumnus and former member of the Brook Farm Transcendentalist community in Massachusetts, observed that "merriment & exhilaration are almost sure to take the lead over rivalry & anxiety."[19]

Baseball, however, was also a game of skill, and not everyone could play it. Despite A. G. Spalding's protestations that baseball was a democratic game, some individuals, such as Horace Greeley, editor of the *New-York Tribune*, and John Howard Raymond, president of Vassar College, confessed their ineptitude for baseball. In any event, Henry Chadwick believed that those who excelled in the "moral attributes" of the game were just as important as those who demonstrated "physical superiority."[20]

As befits a game with vernacular origins, baseball was played under different rules in different venues. The Massachusetts game was a bit unruly, its distinguishing feature being the provision that striking a runner between bases with a thrown ball—known in Ontario, where it was also practiced, as "soaking"—would produce an out. Baseball as played in Massachusetts also featured overhand pitching as opposed to the practice of tossing the ball underhand, like horseshoes, from pitcher to batter.

The Massachusetts game eventually faded out of favor. It's tempting, and not entirely implausible, to suppose that a growing number of bruised players, plunked once too often during their transit between bases, agitated for less punishing rules. But baseballs were softer and lighter then, which meant decreased velocity on throws, and there is no evidence that anyone was seriously injured under this provision of the rules.[21]

The version of baseball that emerged as the preferred game was played in and around New York City. Organized teams had played a form of baseball in New York as early as 1823, and in September 1845 the Knickerbocker Base Ball Club of New York codified twenty rules for baseball. The rules standardized the distance between bases, stipulated that a regulation game consisted of seven innings (six outs to an inning, three for each side), and decreed that the batter was out if the ball was caught on the fly or on the first bounce (the latter provision was eliminated by 1865). Rule 17 stated simply, "All disputes and differences relative to the game, to be decided by the Umpire, from which there is no appeal." Significantly, the Knickerbocker rules forbade balls being thrown at the runner and stipulated that balls hit outside of the lines extending from home to first and from home to third base and beyond would be ruled foul.[22]

Although he has been erroneously identified as the true progenitor of baseball, Alexander Joy Cartwright nevertheless played a role in the early development of the game. Born in New York City in 1820, Cartwright was a volunteer firefighter and worked first as a bank clerk and later as a bookseller before heading to California in the Gold Rush of 1849 and eventually to Hawai'i. Cartwright helped to organize the Knickerbocker Base Ball Club in 1845, which originally played in Madison Square and then in Murray Hill; because of diminishing space in Manhattan due to development, they eventually relocated the games to a bucolic setting called the Elysian Fields, named for the most heroic and virtuous souls in Greek mythology, a six-cent ferry ride across the Hudson River in Hoboken, New Jersey. The first game involving players beyond members of the club itself took place on June 19, 1846, a matchup between the Knickerbocker Club and the New York Club. The Knickerbockers lost 23–1. According to Duncan Curry, president of the Knickerbocker Club, the reason for the shellacking was that the New Yorkers were skilled and clever cricketeers, their pitcher delivered "an awfully speedy ball," and the Knickerbockers, underestimating their opponents, had neglected to practice. Stung by their defeat, the Knickerbockers did not play in Hoboken again until 1851, five years later.[23]

Baseball began to spread throughout North America in the latter half of the nineteenth century, and it became an international phenomenon. Teams from Maine and Massachusetts played teams from the Maritimes; Québécois squared off against teams from Vermont and New Hampshire. Teams from the Great Lakes states played against teams from Ontario, Manitobans faced teams from Minnesota and the Dakotas, plains leagues spanned the border, and players from British Columbia faced off against teams from the Pacific Northwest. Baseball came to the South principally through the agency of the Civil War. Although it was played sporadi-cally in the South prior to what Southerners called the War Between the States, the real catalyst was the war itself, when Union army prisoners introduced baseball to Confederate soldiers or Union army occupation troops demonstrated the game to civilians.[24]

Baseball, especially as it evolved in the latter decades of the nineteenth century, developed into a game of paradoxes. Indeed, a paradox lies at the center of baseball: the fundamental confrontation between pitcher and batter that serves as the catalyst for action in the game. As anyone who has played baseball at the highest levels will attest, success depends on negotiating a synthesis between concentration and relaxation. "A full mind is an empty bat," Branch Rickey once remarked. The inimitable Yogi Berra acknowledged much the same thing: "You can't think and hit at the same time." Stan Musial, another Hall of Famer, understood the paradox slightly differently, arguing that "the secret of hitting is phys-ical relaxation, mental concentration—and don't hit the fly ball to cen-ter." Whatever the formulation, a hitting coach knows when the batter is concentrating too hard when he observes him clenching the handle of the bat. So too with a pitching coach and a pitcher gripping the ball. Both pitcher and batter must simultaneously combine mental focus with physical insouciance. This paradox of concentration and relaxation, what George F. Will describes as a ballplayer's "peculiar equilibrium," lies at the very heart of the game.[25]

Beyond this central paradox, however, the structure, meaning, and symbolism of baseball itself emerge from three larger paradoxes; taken together, they help us understand the game. First is the paradox that a game with apparent roots in America's emerging premier metropolitan area nevertheless celebrates bucolic virtues. Second, the paradox that a game born in the teeth of the Industrial Revolution nevertheless flouts industrialism's central organizing principle: the regulation of time. Finally, the paradox that a game that boasts its putative indigenous ori-gins nevertheless embodies and, in many ways, replicates the experience of immigrants and outsiders.

The challenge of playing a bucolic game in an urban setting presented itself early in the history of baseball. The weekly newspaper *Spirit of the*

Times reported in 1856 that every empty lot within a ten-mile radius of New York City was being used as a baseball field. In the run-up to the 1862 season, the *Brooklyn Eagle* noted that several teams were scrambling to find places to play and that the field on Fifth Avenue in Manhattan would likely not be used much because of the encroachment of buildings. "The great disadvantage attached to the Ball Clubs—which every year is increasing—is that of procuring grounds," the article continued. "The vacant lots and unfenced fields in the suburban districts and the vicinity of the city are every year becoming in more demand." The "Green Monster" in Fenway Park in Boston provides continuing testimony to the constraints of urban space. In New York City, several teams found greener pastures across the Hudson.[26]

A flight into the airport of nearly any American city illustrates the incongruity of baseball in an urban setting: A few islands of green punctuate the cityscape, which is often defined by concrete canyons and dun-colored streets. Novelist Philip Roth described Sunday afternoons at Ruppert Stadium in Newark, New Jersey, "a green wedge of pasture miraculously walled in among the factories, warehouses, and truck depots of industrial Newark." I remember clearly my first visit to Tiger Stadium in Detroit in the mid-1960s—coming off the gritty streets, walking through the tunnel, and beholding the verdant, piercing beauty of the field. Tom Stanton described a similar feeling many years later in his elegy to the same stadium in its final season as home of the Tigers. "Emerging from the cement tunnel you notice the grass first, shamrock green," he writes, adding that "green represents youth, vitality, and promise and they abound at a ballpark, in our spirits and minds if nowhere else."[27]

We can well imagine that the grass of a baseball field provided a welcome respite for the weary industrial workers of the nineteenth century, an escape from the drudgeries of industrialism. For some, it served as a reminder of their own rural upbringing. For others, it provided an invitation to imagine what lay beyond the serrated skyline and the congestion of the city. The durability of the Cooperstown myth might be explained in part by its assertion of the game's pastoral origins and the allure of a faded bucolic past.[28]

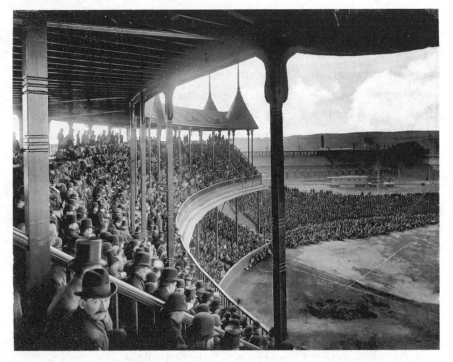

The Grand Pavilion at South End Grounds, Boston, with industry in the distance, illustrating the disjunction between the verdant fields of baseball and the Industrial Revolution. National Baseball Hall of Fame and Museum, Cooperstown, N.Y.

As for the field itself, the bases correspond to the four cardinal points of the compass. The outfield stretches indeterminately, and I'm intrigued by the possibility that the boundaries of the outfield matched contemporary notions of the frontier. Early ball fields did not have outfield fences; a batted ball theoretically could roll forever. After the 1890 census declared the American frontier closed, outfields began to be delimited, albeit still in uncertain terms. The outfield boundaries in older American ballparks (as well as in more recent ballparks that seek to replicate the charm of earlier ones) are uneven and irregular, reflecting the uncertainty at the time about what lay to the West.

If the baseball field offered a contrast to the urbanism emerging in American society, its disposition toward time was positively countercultural.

Over the course of the nineteenth century, the clock became the icon of the Industrial Revolution. With the emergence of textile mills, factories, and professional offices, workers suddenly oriented their lives away from the circadian rhythms of the seasons—working in daylight hours and sleeping at night—and toward the demands of their employers. The clock, not daylight, regulated their lives, sleeping and waking; bosses showed little tolerance for someone who did not begin work at the specified hour.

Baseball is the only major sport not governed by a clock. As such, it hearkens back to a more idyllic time when we were not bullied by the tyranny of time. The absence of a clock in baseball, as A. Bartlett Giamatti, former commissioner of baseball, said, "keeps time fat and slow and lazy." Even the baserunner circles the bases *counterclockwise*, as though baseball seeks to subvert the passage of time.[29]

These days, the conservators of baseball worry that the game is too slow; perhaps, they say, a clock will speed it up and generate interest from younger fans. In the nineteenth century, however, baseball was regarded as a vast improvement over cricket, "purely an English game," according to the *Brooklyn Eagle*, one that "never will be in much vogue with the Americans, especially New Yorkers, who are all for fast and not slow things." Jacob Morse, in his 1888 history of baseball, concurred, arguing that cricket was "too slow, too leisurely, for the American."[30]

In baseball, however, time is measured not so much in minutes or hours as in seasons, and the baseball season itself follows an agricultural calendar: planting in the spring, cultivation in the summer, harvest in the autumn. Giamatti again: "It breaks your heart. It is designed to break your heart. The game begins in the spring, when everything else begins again, and it blossoms in the summer, filling the afternoons and evenings, and then as soon as the chill rains come, it stops and leaves you to face the fall all alone. You count on it, rely on it to buffer the passage of time, to keep the memory of sunshine and high skies alive, and then just when the days are all twilight, when you need it most, it stops."[31]

The final defining paradox of baseball is that despite the efforts of Spalding and others to assert its purely American origins, baseball provides a metaphor for the immigrant experience and for those on the margins of American society. Baseball's sorry history of excluding African Americans hardly needs to be rehearsed here to make the point that, despite their demonstrated talent, Blacks struggled for admission into professional leagues. Jackie Robinson's debut with the Brooklyn Dodgers on April 15, 1947, initiated the desegregation of the major leagues, a process that would take a dozen years to complete, when the Boston Red Sox finally became the last major league team to add an African American player to its roster.[32]

The struggle to incorporate "outsiders" into the game of baseball, however, began much earlier. Bud Fowler, whom the *Lawrence (Kansas) Evening Tribune* described as "the phenomenal colored player of Topeka," competed against white teams in the 1880s until the International League formally barred Black players in 1887. Native Americans were playing baseball on reservations, at the Carlisle Indian Industrial School, and as far away as Alaska in the waning decades of the nineteenth century. On April 22, 1897, Louis Francis Sockalexis, a Penobscot, became first player of Native American descent to play professional baseball when he broke in with the Cleveland Spiders as a right fielder (his presence may have prompted the Cleveland team to change its name to "Indians" in 1915). Elijah Edward Pinnance, a Chippewa, was the first full-blooded American Indian to play in a major league game when he pitched for the Philadelphia Athletics against the Washington Senators on September 14, 1903. These players were followed by dozens of others, including Jim Thorpe and Charles Albert "Chief" Bender, who was elected to the Hall of Fame in 1953. But these Native Americans were considered outsiders, the subject of catcalls, war whoops, and the inevitable nickname "Chief." A Cleveland sportswriter reported that Sockalexis was "hooted at and howled at by the thimble-brained brigade on the bleachers." Following Pinnance's appearance, a prominent white player was quoted as saying, apparently with no hint of irony, "I don't think it looks right for these foreigners to be breaking into the game."[33]

Although Native Americans clearly had a claim to being "American," Jews, Blacks, and others were still considered outsiders. The House of David, a utopian, millenarian community based in Benton Harbor, Michigan, fielded a team of cultural outcasts, Jewish and otherwise, that barnstormed throughout the Midwest and beyond in the early decades of the twentieth century. Mormons in the Mountain West played base-ball as a way of demonstrating their identity as Americans. Hank Green-berg, the "Hebrew Hammer," played in the major leagues from 1933 to 1947, with a four-year interruption for military service in World War II (he was the first major league player to enlist). Like Native Americans before him, Greenberg faced racial taunts. During the Detroit Tigers' 1935 World Series against the Chicago Cubs, the stream of vitriol from the Cubs' dugout directed against Greenberg was so vile and incessant that the home-plate umpire threatened to eject the offending players on the Cubs' bench. "How the hell could you get up to home plate every day and have some son of a bitch call you a Jew bastard and a kike and a sheenie," Greenberg recalled, "without feeling the pressure. If the ball-players weren't doing it, the fans were."[34]

African Americans were in many ways the ultimate outsiders. As attested by the success and the quality of play in the Negro Leagues, African Americans excelled at baseball, even though they were denied the opportunity to play in the major leagues. In 1933 at the annual din-ner for baseball writers in New York City, Heywood Broun, sportswriter and unsuccessful Socialist candidate for Congress three years earlier, said he saw no reason Blacks should not be allowed to play major league baseball. Jimmy Powell, sportswriter for the *New York Daily News*, infor-mally polled some of the baseball figures at the same dinner; only John McGraw, manager of the New York Giants, objected to Blacks playing in the major leagues.[35]

The cause of racial integration was taken up by others, including Wal-ter Winchell and several Jewish sportswriters. But the real impetus behind the desegregation of baseball might have been Black newspapers—the *Chicago Defender*, the *People's Voice*, and the *Pittsburgh Courier-Journal*, the largest Black newspaper in the nation, which crusaded for the cause with editorials, interviews, and feature articles for more than a decade, beginning in 1933. During a meeting with Branch Rickey on April 17, 1945, Wendell Smith, sports editor of the *Courier-Journal* who himself was denied an opportunity to play in the major leagues, told the general manager of the Brooklyn Dodgers that a young shortstop for the Kansas City Monarchs had what it takes to play major league baseball. Rickey, a devout Methodist with strict Sabbatarian scruples (he would not watch

Jackie Robinson (1919–1972) and Branch Rickey (1881–1965), general manager of the Brooklyn Dodgers. Rickey, a devout Methodist, said that promoting Robinson to the major leagues was "the most important thing I ever did in my life." New York Daily News Archive via Getty Images.

even his own teams on Sunday), eventually pursued Smith's lead. Rickey surreptitiously sent his scouts to assess Jackie Robinson and several other African American players. Rickey, who had a portrait of Abraham Lincoln in his office, signed Robinson to a minor league contract and then promoted him to the Dodgers two years (almost to the day) after his meeting with Smith. Rickey told a reporter that his decision to elevate Robinson to the major leagues was "the most important thing I ever did in my life."[36]

Robinson's struggle has been well documented. He faced long odds against the entrenched racism of fans and fellow players, enduring epithets, death threats, and more than a few indignities along the way. Like the immigrants and the Native Americans before him, Robinson was an outsider playing a game that replicates the experience of outsiders.[37]

Baseball is the only game where the *defense* controls the ball, and it is the mission of the offensive player (the hitter) to disrupt the defense's control of the ball. The batter is outnumbered nine to one against a defense malevolently configured to foil his efforts. The pitcher, his immediate adversary, seeks to thwart him with a bewildering array of pitches that spin, fade, curve, dart, slow, or accelerate. The odds are against him, just as they were for Robinson and other African Americans both in society and in baseball itself. A batter successful only three times out of ten—who therefore fails more than twice as often as he succeeds—likely will head to the Hall of Fame. "Where else in life can you fail that often and be a success?" Al Kaline of the Detroit Tigers asked rhetorically; he added, "Baseball is a game that you measure in failure."[38]

Immigrants and outsiders nevertheless have both watched and played the game. "Particularly for men, and especially commonly for Jewish men," Stephen Jay Gould noted about baseball, "a dedication to a distinctly American sport provides the major tactic for assimilation." Many outsiders have excelled at the game itself. A glance at the rosters of early baseball reveals the surnames of immigrants—O'Neill, Comiskey, Orr, Roseman, Penno, Keiger, Milligan, Stivetts, Hogriever, O'Brien, Lachance, Zimmer—people who, more likely than not, were struggling to find their place in American society. Philip Roth recalled seeing African Americans in the stands at a Newark Bears game, along with the city's Germans, Irish, and Poles.[39]

The field that lay before them as they peered from the batter's box was hostile territory. That alien world contained only three islands of safety—first, second, and third base—as the batter sought to negotiate his against-all-odds, counterclockwise circuit. The batter's ultimate, elusive goal was to return safely home, just as the immigrant fantasizes about returning to his homeland in triumph or the little boy in the 1744 *Little Pretty Pocket Book* flees "Home with Joy." And often as not, like Odysseus returning from his travels, the batter can regale his mates with tales of his adventure.

Immigrants and other outsiders—Irish, Germans, Italians, African Americans, Jews, and, more recently, Latinos and Asians—have always played and sometimes excelled at baseball, America's ostensibly indigenous game. Like the batter himself, they defied the odds and carved a

Baseball, the quintessential immigrant game, has always appealed to those who might be considered outsiders—and they, in turn, have often excelled at the game. This July 11, 1949, photograph captures Jackie Robinson (1919–1972), an African American; Sid Gordon (1917–1975), a Jewish American; and Joe DiMaggio (1914–1999), an Italian American. Each represented a New York team: Brooklyn Dodgers, New York Giants, and New York Yankees. Bettmann via Getty Images.

place for themselves on the American landscape. More than any other game, baseball—the game that frequently tried to exclude them—encapsulated their struggles.

Baseball is a game of paradoxes, and its singular achievement through the decades is its durability—despite such adversities as periodic labor unrest, the Black Sox Scandal of 1919, Pete Rose's gambling addiction, the steroid era, and the use of electronics to steal signs. "The one constant through all the years," according to James Earl Jones as the fictional Terrence Mann in *Field of Dreams*, "has been baseball." Although most metrics suggest that football has overtaken baseball in popularity, baseball continues to intrigue, its emerald fields offering a counterpoint to the urban environments in which it is played (at least at the professional level). In that sense, and also in the sense that baseball continues even in the twenty-first century to resist the marking of time, baseball is countercultural.[40]

Because baseball is countercultural and its apologists prone to rhapsodizing and mythologizing, various pundits and scholars have sought to assign religious significance to the structure of the game. Some see the pitcher's mound, the highest point on the field, as a cosmic mountain and the mythical center of the field, the point of creation from which all play originates. Others note the trinitarian nature of three outs to a half inning or three times three for the number of players and innings. Mircea Eliade's *Myth of the Eternal Return* figures into many of these analyses as well as such durable religious notions as faith, doubt, and redemption.[41]

Some students of Buddhism insist that the numerology of baseball replicates Buddhist principles: three (strikes, jewels, vehicles); four (balls, bases, noble truths); nine (players, innings, *yanas*). Helen Tworkov, one such student, cited Abner Doubleday's affiliation with the Theosophical Society to suggest that Doubleday's familiarity with Buddhism impelled him to embed these characteristics into the game. Apparently unmoved by the fact that Doubleday did *not* invent baseball, Tworkov goes on to point out that the shape of the field may be a reference to the *Diamond Sutra* and that the number of stitches on a baseball, 108, is also the total of $3 \times 4 \times 9$, "the same number of Buddhist prayer beads on a sacred mala as well as the number used ritually and repeatedly throughout Buddhist cultures."[42]

In less esoteric religious terms, baseball represents the Garden of Eden, a lost, halcyon paradise—or at least one in perpetual danger of being eclipsed by modern sensibilities. The Mills Commission and the contestation over baseball's origins prefigured contemporary debates over the creation accounts in the book of Genesis—so-called creationists insist that these narratives be interpreted literally—but just as Charles Darwin's evolutionary theory cast a shadow over the Genesis creation narratives, so too a more "scientific" (that is, historical) analysis of the origins of baseball yields a very different, more prosaic, narrative.

Still, the lure of Eden is strong. The baseball field itself evokes a simpler, sylvan past, and when the field is surrounded by a loved and venerable stadium, it becomes, for many, sacred space. The Cooperstown myth, similar to the Genesis creation myth, celebrates the pastoral virtues of a lost America. More than a quarter of a million pilgrims trek to Coopers-town, the mythical birthplace of the game, every year, and another one hundred thousand visit the *Field of Dreams* movie site in Dyersville, Iowa, which offers a similar, Edenic version of baseball.

Even in the Garden of Eden, however, the serpent lurks: persistent racism, labor unrest, owners' collusion, performance-enhancing drugs. The wonder is not that baseball has faced such adversities, several of which are common to other sports, but that it has endured.

At its best, albeit belatedly in far too many instances, baseball wel-comed immigrants and outsiders. Major League Baseball was uncon-scionably delinquent in admitting African Americans into its ranks, and yet Branch Rickey's decision to add Jackie Robinson to the roster of the Brooklyn Dodgers anticipated by more than a year Harry Truman's exec-utive order to integrate the armed forces and antedated by seven years the Supreme Court's landmark *Brown v. Board of Education* decision. The history of professional baseball has been marred by labor disputes, some of them ugly and one-sided in favor of the owners, but the attenuation of the reserve clause late in the twentieth century allowed players, some of whom had grown up in poverty, to partake of baseball's bounty.

Is baseball still America's pastime? In a sense, the question is irrele-vant because baseball cares little about time. It rejected the horological icon of the Industrial Revolution in the nineteenth century, and it contin-ues to resist efforts to speed the pace of the game. Baseball reckons time in seasons or even in decades—the dead-ball era, the Murderers' Row Yankees dynasty, the Big Red Machine—rather than minutes or hours.[43]

"America has rolled by like an army of steamrollers," Terrence Mann concludes in *Field of Dreams*. "It has been erased like a blackboard, rebuilt, and erased again. But baseball has marked the time."[44]

CHAPTER 2

A Great Moral Force

The Civil War and the Origins of Football

Football is a war game. The most remarkable similarity exists between the basic principles of combat in war and in football.

—CHARLES D. DALY

After all, is football a game or a religion?

—HOWARD COSELL

The 1925 meeting of the National Collegiate Athletic Association at the Hotel Astor in New York City pitted two Dartmouth College professors against one another. James P. Richardson, professor of political science and chair of the resolutions committee for the National Collegiate Athletic Association (NCAA), proposed a measure condemning the commercial excesses that surrounded the Rose Bowl football game in Pasadena, California. Such commercialism, Richardson argued, was "detrimental to the best interests of amateur sport." Later, Dartmouth's president, Ernest M. Hopkins, addressed the same gathering on "The Place of Athletics in an Educational Program." Where Richardson sensed danger, Hopkins saw opportunity for the building of character and a hedge against "callow theories of individualism to which many of the undergraduates in American colleges today seem to be particularly susceptible." Hopkins argued that "athletics are a legitimate and a salutary interest of college men, and therefore that their maintenance and control are a legitimate and a desirable responsibility of college officials."[1]

Vigorous moral debates surrounded the development of team sports in North America, and no sport came in for greater scrutiny than football, without question the most violent of the four major sports (hockey has violent eruptions, but violence in football, unlike hockey, is scripted into the game itself). Football was also criticized for its susceptibility to commercialism as well as for the distractions it posed to academic life on campus—criticisms, it hardly needs to be said, that persist to this day.

Andrew Dickson White, president of Cornell, offered perhaps the most withering dismissal of football, in 1874. When students requested leave to play a football game in Cleveland against the University of Michigan, the president refused. "I will not permit thirty men to travel four hundred miles merely to agitate a bag of wind," he declared.[2]

White was hardly football's only critic. Writing in the *North American Review*, George E. Merrill, president of Colgate University, catalogued his specific objections to football and concluded that "any game that has so many elements of unfairness and unfitness should not occupy the first place in the esteem of American youth." Whereas Charles W. Eliot of Harvard declared the "football has become seriously injurious to rational academic life in American schools and colleges," Theodore Roosevelt, a Harvard alumnus, extolled the athletic spirit as "essentially democratic" and warned that eliminating team sports would produce a generation of "mollycoddles."[3]

Football had other defenders. Addressing the Brotherhood of St. Andrew meeting in Baltimore on September 30, 1898, Endicott Peabody, headmaster of the Groton School, extolled the benefits of athletic pursuits. "All athletics are good for boys," he said. "Bicycling is good, tennis is good, baseball is good, and that game is good which a friend of mine calls the most spiritual of all games—football." Peabody continued to enumerate the benefits of the game. Football requires early hours and good nutrition and keeps players from indulging in luxuries, he said. Most of all, football demands obedience; it is an organized game, "and organization is valuable."[4]

Writing in the *North American Review*, J. William White and Horatio C. Wood, both of them professors at the University of Pennsylvania, declared that football "tends to develop self-control, coolness, fertility of resource, and promptness of execution in sudden emergencies." Another commentator, writing the following year, acknowledged that "to stand up to a fast pitched ball, or endure any other trial of nerve with pluck and resolution, is invaluable training." John Franklin Crowell, president of Trinity College (later, Duke University), pronounced himself an "enthusiast" of intercollegiate athletics for its role in "developing the virility, self-control, and daring courage of American youth." Another college president deemed that the advantage of athletics "are unquestionably chiefly moral in their nature," and still another president declared that football "trains in a conspicuous way certain precious elements of character." Isaac Sharpless, president of Haverford College, declared in 1907 that morals had improved over the past twenty-five years because of the development of athletics.[5]

Other observers agreed that exposure to football would have a salutary effect on society, especially morals. "I wish the men in Wall Street, the men who run railroads, would learn something from football," Francis Landey Patton, president of Princeton, told a Sunday school class in Philadelphia in 1898. "In this great fight which we call life it is more than winning—it is the way in which you win." Henry S. Curtis hailed football as "not only a great incentive to effort, an awakener of dormant intellect, but a great moral force as well."[6]

Historians trace some version of "football," where the object is to kick or carry a ball across the end line of a field, back to ancient Mesoamerica, to the Han dynasty in China, and to what are now the Cornwall and Devon areas of England. The ancient Greeks played a game called *phenida*, and the Romans enjoyed *harpaston* (or *harpastum*), both of which involved tackling and the passing of a leather ball. Sports historians often refer to these as "mob games" because of their rambunctious character, with players typically surrounding the ball, and because of the density of players on the field. In 1287, for instance, the Synod of Exeter, in England, deemed it necessary to ban "unseemly sports"—some form of mob game—from churchyards.[7]

Some iteration of football likely migrated to North America with the Pilgrims and the Puritans in the seventeenth century. Back in England, however, rules of the game began to be codified, especially at the Rugby School, in Warwickshire. The students were accustomed to playing

Dartmouth students playing football on the college green, 1880s.
Courtesy of the Dartmouth College Library.

a mob game of football that involved kicking a ball down the field and either touching it down on the other side of the opponents' goal line or drop-kicking the ball over the goal. According to school lore, William Webb Ellis altered the game in 1823 when he elected to run with the ball after catching it, rather than kicking it immediately, as customary. The various iterations of football—rugby—became so popular that on January 26, 1871, representatives of twenty-one clubs met to form the Rugby Union and agree on a common set of rules.[8]

In North America, mob games were popular on college campuses in the nineteenth century, providing a way to dissipate energy and also to reinforce hierarchies among the students. At Harvard, beginning in 1827, sophomores squared off against freshmen in a mob game so violent and unruly that the annual event became known as "Bloody Monday." That same autumn, Dartmouth students played a similar game, which they called the "Usual Game of Football." The game at Dartmouth evolved into what became known as "Old Division" rules, which pitted students of even-numbered class years against odd-numbered class years, presumably making the matchups a bit more equal. The object of the game was to kick the ball "past the east or west fence."[9]

The annual "rough house" game at Yale, a kind of hazing for fresh-men, became so rowdy that in 1858 the town of New Haven barred students from playing on the village green. Two years later, Yale banned the game completely. The faculty at Harvard did the same, prompting the students to conduct a mock funeral for "Football Fightum," a procession complete with a drum major, two bass drums, six pallbearers, and a six-foot coffin with a football inside. The burial solemnities included under-graduate doggerel and a mournful song to the air of "Auld Lang Syne":

> Beneath this sod we lay you down,
> This sign of glorious fight;
> With dismal groans and yells we'll drown
> Your mournful burial rite!

The *Harvard Magazine*, which had called for the elimination of football on campus, was not amused. "No farce or mockery of a burial, however ably contrived, can sink the game lower than it is in the estimation of sensible men," the editorialist huffed, "much less will any crocodile lamentations serve to gull the present or succeeding generations into a belief in the essential purity of the game, or preserve its memory from becoming, as it just should, both odious and abominable."[10]

A mile or so away from the "funeral," however, younger students from elite private schools played football on Boston Common. They played what came to be known as the "Boston Game," twelve players to a team, with scoring by either carrying or kicking the ball beyond the opponents' goal line.[11]

The real impetus for the development of American football, and the event that helped to determine the meaning of the game, was the Civil War, the bellicose tragedy that tallied an estimated three-quarters of a million casualties from April 1861 to April 1865. The battles of the Civil War—Antietam, Chickamauga, Bull Run, Manassas, Gettysburg—were defined by the bloody defense and conquest of territory. The games at America's elite universities, many of them doubtless played by the sons, brothers, and nephews of Civil War officers, mimicked the battlefields of the war just past. The contestation over territory came to define the game.

In 1869, team captain William J. Leggett of Rutgers College, who went on to study theology at New Brunswick Theological Seminary and then to a distinguished career as a minister in the Reformed Church of America, challenged students at the College of New Jersey (Princeton) to a three-game series of football. Prior to the first game, played in New Brunswick on November 6, 1869, with twenty-five players on each team, Leggett and William S. Gummere, the Princeton captain and later chief justice of the New Jersey Supreme Court, negotiated the rules of the game. The Rutgers Queensmen, who wore scarlet-colored bandannas, prevailed 6–4 in a game that featured "headlong running, wild shouting, and frantic kicking," according to the campus newspaper, the *Targum*. "Though smaller on the average, the Rutgers players, as it developed, had ample speed and fine football sense," John W. Herbert recounted. "Receiving the ball, our men formed a perfect interference around it and with short, skillful kicks and dribbles drove it down the field. Taken by surprise, the Princeton men fought valiantly, but in five minutes we had gotten the ball through to our captains on the enemy's goal and S. G. Gano, '71, and G. R. Dixon, '73, neatly kicked it over." A week later and twenty miles to the south, Princeton won. But the rubber match was canceled because of faculty opposition to the violence of the game.[12]

Football, however, was not so easily banished. Columbia joined the New Jersey colleges in 1870, and in 1872 Columbia and Rutgers decided that the ball should be kicked *over* the crossbars, not under. The following year, representatives from Columbia, Princeton, Rutgers, and Yale gathered at the luxurious Fifth Avenue Hotel, on the southwest corner of Madison Square in Manhattan, to hammer out rules for football. There, amid what *Harper's Weekly* described as "heavy masses of gilt wood, rich crimson or green curtains, extremely handsome rose-wood and brocatelle suits," the delegates agreed on the size of the field (400 by 250 feet) and on a provision against throwing or carrying the ball, which would make the play much more like soccer.[13]

Harvard, however, refused to accede to these rules—the captain of the team said they tried them but "gave it up at once as hopeless"—and continued to play the Boston game, which allowed carrying the ball. In 1874, McGill University in Montréal then stepped in with a challenge to Harvard. The teams faced off in Cambridge for a two-game series, with Harvard

William M. Boyd's artistic representation of the first intercollegiate football game, in New Brunswick, New Jersey, on November 6, 1869. Rutgers defeated the College of New Jersey (Princeton) 6–4. Special Collections and University Archives, Rutgers University Libraries.

players wearing "magenta" handkerchiefs for the first time. Harvard won the first game, played under the Boston rules. The second game, played with an oblong ball under rugby rules, ended in a tie. The Harvard men decided that they preferred McGill's rules. On October 23, 1874, Harvard traveled to Montréal for a third game, this one played with rugby-style rules.[14]

In 1876, the nation's centennial, representatives from Princeton, Yale, Columbia, and Harvard met at Massasoit House in Springfield, Massachusetts, during Thanksgiving break to establish a collegiate football association. The oval ball—a leather casing over a rubber bladder—was specified, and the size of the field set at 140 yards by 70 yards. By 1878, twelve colleges were playing in the Intercollegiate Football Association.[15]

For the moment, representatives from Yale lost their bid to reduce the number of players on each team from fifteen to eleven. But Walter Camp,

A representation of the Harvard-McGill football game, played with rugby-style rules at the Montréal Cricket Grounds on October 23, 1874. McCord Museum, Montréal, VIEW-579.A.

a halfback and captain of the Yale football team, pressed his case. Camp, who worked at his family's business, the New Haven Clock Company, also decided that the game needed to be governed by a clock. Whereas baseball had rejected the icon of the Industrial Revolution, Camp and the game of football embraced it.[16]

What Camp hated most about football was the scrum; the heaving mass was too chaotic, the game too dependent on brute force or on the whim of the mob. Camp envisioned a far more strategic game, one where coaches and players could devise elaborate plays and square off neatly. He described football as "a game of strategy, skill and brains, and it appeals to cultured and intelligent people who appreciate what qualities it represents."[17]

The chaotic *scrum* gave way to a line of *scrimmage*; players from opposing teams would line up across from one another at the point where the ball carrier had been tackled to the ground on the previous play. Camp, generally acknowledged as the "father of American football," also introduced the notion of downs, where each team had three opportunities to advance the ball at least five yards or surrender the ball to the opposing team (the interval was elongated to ten yards in 1906). That innovation

Walter Camp (1859–1925), the "father of American
football," 1924. Walter Chauncey Camp Papers (MS
125), Manuscripts and Archives, Yale University Library.

in turn led to a "gridiron" of markers on the field to measure progress. In
1880, Camp finally persuaded his football colleagues to reduce the number of players on a side from fifteen to eleven.[18]

Camp's innovations introduced strategy and reduced the level of
chaos in the game, but they also, perhaps inadvertently, made football
more violent. With teams lined up on opposite sides of a line of scrimmage, they were able to generate momentum as the play began before
running into their opponents. Early descriptions of almost any early football game employ the word "brutality." The rules allowed a player in this
era to hit another player three times with closed fists before he would
be ejected. Teams delighted in obliterating their opponents, sometimes
by triple-digit margins. In 1884, for example, Princeton beat Lafayette
140–0; the Tigers shut out Johns Hopkins 108–0 in 1888 and beat Virginia 115–0 two years later. The faculty at Harvard once again banned the
playing of football in 1885, although it was reinstated the following year.

In 1897, the governor of Georgia, William Yates Atkinson, vetoed a bill that would have outlawed football in Georgia.[19]

Camp relished the introduction of what he called "strategical possibilities" into the game, and he devoted his coaching energies to devising more and more complex schemes to confuse and stymie his opponents. "There is room for an almost infinite number of as yet unthought-of plays," he wrote in 1910. But Camp also recognized football's affinities with what he called the "Game of War" and the "mimic battles of the gridiron." Describing the first game between Army and Navy in 1890, Camp noted that both teams "are making a study of the art of war, and there is no sport known that in its very nature so mimics that art as the game of football. The tactics, the formations, the strategies, the attack and defense, all belong equally to the military commander and the football captain." Elsewhere, Camp spoke about the "generalship of the game" and the "assaulting team." This connection to combat, Camp believed, accounted for the appeal of football. "A certain strain of the fighting blood in the veins of every healthy man and woman," he wrote, "is undoubtedly responsible for one of the elements of the popularity of modern foot ball to many spectators."[20]

W. W. Heffelfinger, one of Camp's players at Yale and a three-time all-American, also extolled the strategic possibilities of football—he compared the game to "a great chess board"—but he recognized the visceral, pugilistic appeal of the game. "Men still like to see personal combat," he wrote in the *Boston Sunday Globe*. "It's in their natures, although the days of hand-to-hand fighting are over." He added: "In no other game is there this direct struggle of man to man."[21]

Charles F. Thwing, president of Abelhert College and Western Reserve University, extolled the virtues of football, including discipline. He compared playing football to military service. "The discipline of the regular United States Army is an education which, if not liberal, is liberating," he wrote in the *Independent*. "The rigor and vigor of football have a similar effect." Other contemporaries recognized the parallels. "War," according to John Prentiss Jr., a fullback, "is the greatest game on earth." A professor at the University of Virginia observed, "If I should pick out a man whom I could follow in peace and war, my choice would be a good football player."[22]

By this time, the developers of football could draw on multiple sources beyond Civil War battlefields for inspiration. The principles of Muscular Christianity—the full armor of God, fighting against the wiles of the devil—had begun to filter across the Atlantic. The best-selling book in nineteenth-century America, the Bible, includes more than three dozen accounts of battles between ancient Israel and the Assyrians or the Midianites or the Canaanites or the Philistines. David marshaled his army to conquer Jerusalem, which later fell to the Babylonians in the Siege of Jerusalem, and Joshua led Israel into battle thirteen times. The history of Christianity itself, the religion that commanded the allegiance of a majority of Americans, was hardly lacking in pugilism.

Perhaps the most explicit linking of football with war came from Charles Dudley Daly. "Football appeals so strongly to the American public because it is a war game," Daly declared; it evokes "the fundamental battle spirit. . . . Its strategy and tactics are those of war." Daly was a quarterback at Harvard, a player Camp described as the "most brilliant individual performer that Harvard has placed upon the gridiron." Daly's own career embodied the connection between football and the military. On the eve of the Harvard-Yale football game in 1900, Daly learned that he had been appointed to the U.S. Military Academy at West Point. After leaving Harvard, he played for two years at West Point (the team's only loss during the 1901 season was to Harvard). He coached football at the academy from 1913 to 1916 and again from 1919 to 1922, compiling a record of 58–13–3.[23]

Daly, as befit his post at Army, gloried in martial metaphors for the game he loved. "A game of football is a battle," he wrote, whose object is "the destruction (figurative) or the overwhelming of the enemy." Daly's 1921 treatise, *American Football*, teases out the connections. "A remarkable similarity exists between war and football," the book begins. "In both war and football we have the staff and the troops. In both we have the supply department, medical branch, and the instruction branch. In both, the importance of leadership is paramount." Both enterprises, he added, seek to capitalize on opponents' weaknesses, and Daly was unsparing in his references to football as combat, arguing that the "great principles of combat in war are the great principles of combat in football." In terms of strategy, as in war, Daly argued, offense was more important than

Charles Dudley Daly (1880–1959) in many
ways personified the link between football and
militarism. He played quarterback for both Harvard
and the U.S. Military Academy and later served
as head coach of the football team at West Point.
History and Art Collection / Alamy Stock Photo.

defense; nevertheless, "each defensive operation, in the classic defense, is a savage attack on the offensive play."[24]

Among his many military metaphors, Daly referred to the "generalship" of the quarterback. Indeed, military nomenclature appeared early in the history of football—training camp, drills, formation, scouts, tactics, strategy—and the language of warfare persists in a game concerned with the conquest and the defense of territory. A team's offense typically is a blend of a "ground game" and an "aerial attack," intended to "invade enemy territory." Game announcers frequently refer to a quarterback as the "field general," who fires "bullet passes" or "long bombs." He often lines up in "shotgun formation," several yards behind the center. A talented running back is "explosive," and a massive rush of defensive players is called a "blitz," short for "blitzkrieg," a German tactic in World War II. Coaches and fans refer to the "gladiator battles" or the "trench warfare" between the offensive and defensive lines, a reference to World War I, and they often insist that the game is won or lost there in the trenches; the team that controls the line of scrimmage often wins the game.[25]

No one exploited the connections between football and war better that Lorin F. Deland, an independently wealthy businessman in Boston who indulged in a number of interests, including military history. A friend invited him to watch a football game in Cambridge. "Instantly I was entertained," he recalled. "It was war. Two armies were being hurled at each other, and I was in my element." Deland traveled to Springfield to watch Yale beat Harvard, "when more than ever I was impressed with the similarity between a scientifically played foot ball game and the art of warfare."[26]

Deland became obsessed. Drawing on his study of military strategy, especially the Napoleonic wars, he spent untold hours devising new plays for football. He struck up a friendship with several Harvard players and persuaded them that his plays would work. His signature scheme, which became known as Deland's Flying Wedge, was unveiled in the 1892 Harvard-Yale game. Harvard lost the game, but the play was effective, even though the team's captain acknowledged that it was poorly executed. Deland explained his strategy as "nothing more or less than the application to foot ball of some of Napoleon's methods for turning the enemy's flank."[27]

The flying wedge, the sports equivalent of a medieval battering ram, ramped up the violence associated with football. The play was outlawed several years later, in 1906, but Deland's insights and contributions to the game epitomized football's connection to warfare.[28]

Aside from the nature of the game itself, even the setting and the trappings surrounding football echo references to war. Soldier Field in Chicago, War Memorial Stadium in Buffalo, and also in Little Rock, Arkansas, or the Los Angeles Memorial Coliseum (a reference to ancient gladiatorial struggles) only begin to tap the bellicose nomenclature of football stadiums. During halftime at most college games, marching bands take the field in elaborate formations, an echo of military bands.

A wood engraving by Winslow Homer, "Holiday in Camp—Soldiers Playing Foot-Ball," illustrates the affinities between football and militarism. This lithograph appeared in the July 15, 1865, issue of *Harper's Weekly*.

And lest anyone miss the point, football contests open with the national anthem, a song inspired by the Battle of Baltimore during the War of 1812, sometimes followed by military jets screaming across the sky.

If football replicated the battlefield, the reverse was also true. Beginning in the 1890s, the military academies recognized the utility of athletics, especially football, both for physical fitness and for teaching the rudiments of warfare. The first Army-Navy football game was played on December 1, 1890, and the West Point team soon became competitive with football powerhouses. One alumnus argued that athletic training would produce "hardened veterans, upon whom the safety of the nation could depend." Football in the military flourished during World War I. "In every army cantonment," *Outside* magazine wrote, "footballs were as thick as pumpkins in an autumn cornfield."[29]

According to several metrics, including revenue and attendance, football is now America's most popular game. But to attain that status, football overcame its white Protestant Northeastern origins to become a national game by expanding to the South, by including Catholics, and by becoming the first of the four sports to be racially integrated. Football, in short, confronted the three Rs: region, religion, and race.[30]

The affinity between football and militarism helps to explain football's extraordinary appeal in the South. As Jim Webb, former secretary of the navy and U.S. senator from Virginia, remarked about his own Scots-Irish heritage in 1997, "We have been soldiers for 2,000 years." He added, "The military virtues have been passed down at the dinner table." This is not a new or a recent observation. "War suits them," William Tecumseh Sherman, the Union general, said about the "young bloods of the South" while camped along the Big Black River in Mississippi in the autumn of 1863; "the rascals are brave, fine riders, bold to rashness, and dangerous subjects in every sense."[31]

A culture of honor and violence, not to mention a concentration of military bases, characterizes the South, so it is not surprising that, according to the U.S. Department of Defense, nearly 44 percent of military recruits hail from the South, even though the South (sixteen states and the District of Columbia) represents only about 36 percent of the population. The devotion to football in the South may be more difficult to quantify, but it is no less real. "We must *know* football to *be* Southern," essayist Rick Bragg wrote in 2012, noting that the real allegiance is to college football rather than professional football because the latter is a relatively new phenomenon. "We are of long memory here," Bragg says about his fellow Southerners, and "college football has been an antidote to an often dark history for as long as even our oldest people can recall." There is no small irony in the fact that a game developed by the sons and nephews of Union army officers after the Civil War, a conflict that generated the "long memory" that Bragg mentioned, became a staple of the South.[32]

The first intercollegiate football game south of the Mason-Dixon line took place at the North Carolina State Fairgrounds in Raleigh on Thanksgiving Day, 1888. Trinity College (now Duke University) squared off against the University of North Carolina before a crowd estimated at five hundred. Trinity was considered the underdog, but the Methodist school beat North Carolina 16–0. Football had been introduced to Trinity by its president, John Franklin Crowell, who was educated at both Dartmouth and Yale, including a year at Yale Divinity School. Crowell had written

John Franklin Crowell (1857–1931), ca. 1897, who
attended Dartmouth and Yale, including a year
at Yale Divinity School, brought football to Trinity
College (now Duke University). He described
the game as "first among those sports in which
the qualities of the soldier are capable of being
developed." Duke University Archives.

about football for the *New Haven Morning News* and the *Yale Daily News*,
and he wasted little time introducing Trinity to the game when he arrived
as president in 1887.[33]

Crowell became an evangelist for football, rhapsodizing about how
the game developed virtues in the students. Football, he said, was "first
among those sports in which the qualities of the soldier are capable of
being developed," and the game was a crucial part of Crowell's plans to
transform Trinity College into a modern educational institution. But
Crowell's aspirations for the college, and especially for football, encountered strong resistance from Methodist officials. In late 1892, the Western
Conference of the Methodist Episcopal Church, South, in North Carolina
declared that intercollegiate football was a "source of evil, and no little

evil" and should be abolished immediately. By the middle of 1894, Crowell had submitted his resignation; his successor declared that football was "unfit to be played by young men at college, especially at a Christian College." Although students protested the discontinuation of football, the new president held firm. Trinity lost its final game, 28–0, to the University of North Carolina.[34]

How did football finally gain a toehold in the Old Confederacy? Unsurprisingly, any narrative about football in the South inevitably traverses Alabama. George Petrie, a native of Montgomery, Alabama, and the son of a Presbyterian minister and Confederate chaplain, attended the University of Virginia and earned the PhD from Johns Hopkins University. There he met and befriended Charles Herty, a chemistry student. Both Petrie and Herty became enamored of what was then known as "scientific football" (to distinguish it from soccer) during their time in Baltimore and resolved to introduce it to the South as part of an effort to import progressive, Northern values. Petrie returned to Alabama in 1891 as professor of history at the Agricultural and Mechanical College of Alabama, now Auburn University, and formed a football team; Herty did the same at the University of Georgia. The following February, the two friends organized the first major collegiate football game in the Deep South, thereby initiating the storied Auburn-Georgia rivalry.[35]

The game itself took place in the rain on the afternoon of February 20, 1892. The *Atlanta Journal* estimated the crowd at three thousand, including the Georgia fans who packed into five railroad cars chartered by Southern Railway for the trip from Athens to Atlanta. The entire train was bedecked in red and black. On the muddy field in Atlanta's Piedmont Park, Auburn scored all its points in the second half to upset Georgia 10–0. Petrie later remarked, "Not often, if ever, have I been as happy as I was when that game was over." On that rainy afternoon, however, football had further expanded its reach from the Northeast to the South.[36]

The fans of the University of Alabama, in Tuscaloosa, only 160 miles distant from Auburn, tell a different, complementary story. W. G. Little of Livingston, Alabama, who had attended what became the University of Alabama before transferring to Phillips Academy in Massachusetts, returned to Alabama in 1892 because of the death of his younger brother. Little brought with him a pair of cleats, a leather helmet, an oblong ball,

The beginnings of the Auburn-Georgia rivalry took place in Atlanta's Piedmont Park on February 20, 1892. Agricultural and Mechanical College (now Auburn) defeated the University of Georgia 10–0. Auburn University Libraries Special Collection and Archives.

and tales of a game played in the North. He formed a football team, the Cadets, at the university; the team won its first game, against players from high schools in Birmingham, but finished its inaugural season at 2–2, including a loss to Auburn. A correspondent to the *Birmingham Weekly* was positively giddy about the "magnificent" new game. "Base ball is child's play to football," he wrote in anticipation of the Alabama-Auburn game in 1893. "Instead of one or two men batting or running, imagine twenty-two stout, knotted frames struggling, swaying, pushing, pulling at one great leather ball with the vim and fury of twenty-two tigers."[37]

Alabama trustees, however, were squeamish about the new game, fearing that it would compromise the school's academic reputation. They permitted only one contest in 1897, and the following year Alabama fielded no team at all. The trustees finally relented, and by 1915 Alabama boasted its first all-American, W. T. "Bully" Van de Graaff, who when his ear was badly mutilated in a game against Tennessee two years earlier tried to yank it off completely so he could continue playing. The Alabama team, by then known as the Crimson Tide, traveled to Philadelphia in 1922 and upset the University of Pennsylvania 9–7, the first time a Southern team had prevailed over a Northeastern powerhouse. The Alabama players sang "Dixie" to celebrate their triumph, and they were greeted by a band and hailed as heroes when they returned to Tuscaloosa. On the gridiron in Philadelphia, the South had finally extracted a small measure of revenge against the North.[38]

Among Southerners, the affinities between football and the Civil War are more than coincidental. According to Southern historian Wayne Flynt, George Petrie, who founded the team at Auburn, believed that "football offered Southern men a chance to assert their masculinity and the South's physical supremacy short of actually taking up arms." J. M. Bandry, a professor at Trinity College (Duke University), described football players as "the sons of men who fought in the charge of Pickett and Pettigrew at Gettysburg; or men who laid down their arms with Lee at Appomattox." Bandry saw the phenomenon in generational terms. "As their fathers learned of themselves and their leaders how to fight," he said, "so have these young men learned of themselves and their leaders how to play football." Contests against Northern schools, increasingly defined as anywhere outside of the South, came to be seen as opportunities to revisit the battlefields of Gettysburg or Shiloh in hopes of a different outcome.[39]

Football in the South finally came into its own at the Rose Bowl, in Pasadena, California, on New Year's Day, 1926. Alabama's undefeated record in 1925 earned the team an invitation to Pasadena to play the Washington Huskies, marking the first time that a team from the South competed in the Rose Bowl. Wallace Wade, then in his third year as coach, and his team boarded a train for California with their equipment and with a chip on their shoulders, fully aware that they were bearing the hopes of an entire region. "Alabama's glory is in your hands," the state's governor, William W. Brandon, admonished. "May each member of your team turn his face to the sun-kissed hills of Alabama and fight like hell as did your sires in bygone days." The president of Auburn, Alabama's rival, reminded the Crimson Tide what was at stake: "You are defending the honor of the South," he wrote, "and God's not gonna let you lose this game." The sports editor of the *Atlanta Georgian* wrote that Alabama carried "the reputation of an entire section" of the country. Even the players at Tuskegee Institute registered their support. The Alabama team arrived at the Huntington Hotel in Pasadena to find a telegram from

Johnny Mack Brown (1904–1974), left, running with the football at the Rose Bowl game on January 1, 1926. Alabama beat the University of Washington 20–19. The University of Alabama Libraries Special Collections.

the "Tuskegee Institute Football Team, National Colored Champions." It read, "Huck and Shuck The Huskies."[40]

The Crimson Tide fell behind 12–0 by halftime. In the second half, however, as Southerners back home huddled by telegraph offices, Johnny Mack Brown, a halfback from Dothan, Alabama, described by one writer as "slicker than an eel in a sea of stewed okra," slithered though the Huskies' defense. His sixty-three-yard touchdown reception sealed a 20–19 upset of Alabama over Washington. The *Atlanta Georgian* described the victory as "the greatest victory for the South since the first battle of Bull Run." Southern newspapers resorted to religious language, describing the victory as a "miracle" and "a blessed event." Even the coach of rival Vanderbilt recognized the redemptive nature of Alabama's victory. "Alabama was our representative fighting against the world," he said. "I fought, bled, died, and was resurrected with the Crimson Tide."[41]

Football, for whites at least, had arrived in the South.

Having breeched a geographical barrier, football, a military game invented and developed at Protestant colleges in the Northeast, now faced a religious frontier. The University of Notre Dame had been playing football since 1887; its first game was an 8–0 loss to the University of Michigan Wolverines. After finally beating Michigan in 1909, the Wolverines refused to play Notre Dame for the ensuing thirty-three years.

In 1913, Jesse Harper, head coach at Notre Dame, arranged a game with the Army Black Knights, at West Point. On November 1, the Fighting Irish beat Army by deploying a solid running game coupled with forward passes from quarterback Gus Dorais to Knute Rockne, who contrary to prior convention, which saw the receiver come to a full stop to receive the throw, caught the quarterback's passes in full stride. Notre Dame won 35–13.

With the exception of 1918 (during World War I), the Army–Notre Dame matchup continued annually until 1946; the final game ended in a scoreless tie. For the first decade of the rivalry, the games were played at West Point, but in 1923 Notre Dame alumni persuaded the university's president to shift the contest to New York City, first to Ebbets Field, then to the Polo Grounds, and finally to the newly opened Yankee Stadium. Wall Street bankers and politicians, including Jimmy Walker, mayor of New York, showed up at the games, along with Patrick Joseph Hayes, the archbishop, and priests in Roman collars. Attendance climbed toward eighty thousand, and the annual event became known as the Big Game. The CBS and NBC radio networks broadcast play-by-play accounts of the game.[42]

By then Rockne had taken over as head coach, and the Fighting Irish, behind the famous "Four Horsemen," emerged as a football power. The competitive newspaper environment of the 1920s prompted New York papers to give increased attention to Notre Dame football. A growing number of alumni—Roman Catholics—were living and working in New York City, and Catholics were finally coming into their own. By 1928 Alfred E. Smith, who grew up in the Fulton Street Market and worked his way up through the Tammany Hall machine to become governor of New York, won the Democratic nomination for president, the first Roman Catholic on a major party ticket.

The success of Notre Dame at football—followed by the success of other Catholic schools: Fordham, Boston College, and others—allowed

Catholics finally to beat the Protestants at their own game. American Catholics took vicarious satisfaction in football victories. "ND football has always meant more than just football to me," a Notre Dame alumnus and the grandson of Italian immigrants wrote. "It is a symbol of a people and a way of life."[43]

American Catholics came to understand a win at football both as manifestation of divine favor and as confirmation of their own rising status in American society. As one Notre Dame fan declared, "Notre Dame really did represent the epitome of a Catholic from the South Side of Chicago getting out and making it." After bruising encounters with nativism in the nineteenth century, American Catholics by the middle decades of the twentieth century were winning a measure of grudging acceptance in American society, but the battle, like the proxy battles on the gridiron, had been fierce. "The world is out there, waiting to defeat you," Robert Griffin, a priest and sometime chaplain to the football team at Notre Dame, wrote. "The nameless forces seem arrayed against you on a single field, but you face it as a team trained in the stratagems of victory." The accouterments of religion—prayers, saints' medals, masses—were crucial not only in football but in life. As the priest noted, "Because you are not alone in a hostile universe, you ritualize the battle." The *Catholic Sun*, published in Syracuse, New York, described Notre Dame football as "a kind of sacramental."[44]

Both in substance and symbolism, the Catholic influence in sports extends far beyond football. For example, I've come to see sports radio as a form of auricular confession, the Catholic sacrament of penance when a parishioner enters the confessional to recount his transgressions. Using this rubric, the phenomenon of sports radio can be understood in religious terms, with the host playing the role of cleric. Sports radio opens with the host offering a soliloquy or commentary, very much like a homily or a meditation. Similarly, the bulk of the broadcast is akin to the Catholic practice of auricular confession. A parishioner enters the confessional and says, "Bless me, Father, for I have sinned; it has been six months since my last confession." One of the most familiar incantations in sports radio, especially in the early years, is not all that different. The caller opens with a greeting to the host, "Hi, Mike," and then, "First time, long time," shorthand for first-time caller, long-time listener. What follows, once again, is formulaic. The caller declares himself (almost always male) a "hard-core Dodgers fan," or "big-time Rangers fan" (no one, it seems, is a "small-time" or even a casual fan). The banter that ensues typically consists of the caller offering an observation about his favorite team or a hated rival and asking, either explicitly or indirectly, for the host's agreement or approbation.

As in the confessional, the authority rests entirely with the "priest," the talk-show host, who offers an immediate verdict on the legitimacy of the caller's observation. At times, the host can be withering in his rejoinder, but occasionally he agrees or even acknowledges that the caller—the supplicant—raises a point that even he, the authority, had never considered. This circumstance, albeit rare, provides validation to the caller. Some sports-radio hosts even provide a "caller of the day" feature, which showcases the day's best comment.

Throughout the interactions, however, the lines of authority are clear. The host is the authority. A caller may challenge that authority, but he does so from the position of supplicant. It is no accident that Mike Francesa, arguably the most popular sports-radio host in the nation, was known, not always affectionately, as the "pope."

Beyond region and religion, football faced one final barrier—race—in its quest for universal popularity, an obstacle it negotiated with relative ease in comparison with other team sports. At the professional level, Charles W. Follis became the first African American player when he played for the Shelby (Ohio) Athletic Club on September 15, 1904. When representatives of eleven teams met at Ralph Hay's Hupmobile Agency, in Canton, Ohio, on September 17, 1920, to form the American Professional Football Association, they chose a Native American, the incomparable Jim Thorpe, as league president. Two years later, the association changed its name to National Football League. At that time, the Oorang Indians, a team named for Oorang Dog Kennels in Marion, Ohio, joined the league, a team comprised entirely of Native Americans, including Thorpe.[45]

African Americans had a tougher time. In 1916, Fritz Pollard, a running back, vanquished football powerhouses at Yale, Harvard, and Rutgers to lead Brown University to the Rose Bowl. After college, Pollard coached football at Lincoln University, a historically Black school, and played professional football to maintain his physical conditioning. In November 1919, Ralph "Fat" Waldsmith, owner and coach of the Akron Indians, asked Pollard to play a game against Massillon, the beginning of Pollard's peripatetic career in what became the National Football League.[46]

Though barred from the team's locker room because of his race, Pollard became coach of the Akron Indians, and in 1921 he recruited the all-American Paul Robeson to the Akron team, even though Robeson was simultaneously pursuing his singing and acting careers in addition to studying law at Columbia University. Robeson and Pollard moved on to Milwaukee the following year, where Pollard signed a third Black player, Frederick "Duke" Slater, from the University of Iowa. In 1923, Pollard again coached and played with two African Americans, John Shelburne, an alumnus of Dartmouth, and Jay Mayo "Inky" Williams, Pollard's erstwhile teammate at Brown—this time for the Hammond, Indiana, NFL team. In 1925, Pollard played and coached for three different NFL teams.[47]

All told, thirteen African Americans played in the National Football League between 1920 and 1933. At the end of the 1933 season, however, NFL owners, including George Halas, Art Rooney, and Tim Mara, established a color line. Most evidence suggests that George Preston Marshall, owner of the Boston (later, Washington) Redskins, insisted on the policy, but Pollard claimed that Halas "was the greatest foe of black football players." The exclusion of African American players from the NFL persisted until after World War II, when Kenny Washington, who had been Jackie Robinson's teammate on the UCLA football team, signed with the Los Angeles Rams in 1946. Marshall was finally forced to integrate the Washington Redskins in 1962 under pressure from Stewart Udall, John F. Kennedy's secretary of the interior and effectively the Redskins' landlord at D.C. Stadium. During the 1960s, coincident with the civil rights movement, the number of Black football players in the NFL began to increase dramatically; from 1960 to 1997, the percentage of African American players on NFL rosters rose from 12 percent to 67 percent.[48]

Racial desegregation in college football proceeded—or not—along regional lines, with colleges in the North allowing, even recruiting, African American players while Southern schools resisted. Beginning at the turn of the twentieth century, a so-called gentlemen's agreement obtained by which Northern teams would not allow their Black players to compete when opposing schools from the South. Sometimes, teams resorted to euphemism to justify the exclusion of Black athletes; in the 1929 contest against the University of Georgia, for instance, New York University physicians concocted a diagnosis of "damaged acromiclavicular ligament" to sideline their African American star, Dave Myers.[49]

College football's color line started to recede in the 1930s, beginning with a contest between NYU and the University of North Carolina in 1936 and a subsequent game between Duke and Syracuse two years later. The former took place, with the blessing of UNC's president, Frank Porter Graham, at the Polo Grounds in New York City and featured NYU's African American running back Ed Williams; the game at Syracuse pitted the famous "Iron Duke" defense against Syracuse's Black quarterback, Wilmeth Sidat-Singh. Writing in the *New York Amsterdam News*, the city's preeminent Black paper, Roy Wilkins noted the absence of boos and catcalls against NYU's Ed Williams, adding that "the University of North Carolina is still standing and none of the young men representing it on the gridiron appears to be any worse off for having spent an afternoon competing against a Negro player."[50]

For the Duke-Syracuse game in 1938, Duke coach Wallace Wade, who had led Alabama to its Rose Bowl victory in 1926, was seeking legitimacy. Duke had risen to a top-ten ranking during the course of the 1938 season, and Wade was eager to burnish the team's standing in hopes of another Rose Bowl invitation. To do so, he needed a victory against Syracuse, but beating the Orangemen without their stellar (Black) quarterback, Sidat-Singh, would do nothing to enhance Duke's ranking. "If he doesn't play," Wade told his superiors at Duke, "no matter what the score is, we'll get no credit for winning." The Duke defense shut down Syracuse; Sidat-Singh left the game with an injury in the first quarter, and Duke prevailed 21–0, rising to number five in national rankings.[51]

With these games during the 1930s, the gentlemen's agreement began to wobble, especially for Southern teams in border states and to the West. More and more Southerners took a pragmatic approach to Black athletes: Either they could help your team win, or beating a team with an African American player could redound to the reputation of your team.

Greg Page (1948–1967) broke the color barrier
in the Southeastern Conference, together with
his teammate Nate Northington, in 1967. During
practice, however, Page's teammates piled on
and left him paralyzed. He died thirty-eight days
later. University of Kentucky, Special Collection
Research Center.

Despite episodic advances in the desegregation of college football,
however, Jim Crow maintained a tenacious hold in the South. Greg Page,
a quiet, soft-spoken man, arguably broke the color barrier in the Southeastern Conference when he walked onto the practice field for the University of Kentucky in 1967. In filling out a questionnaire, Page wrote that
he had chosen Kentucky "to help open the way for more Negro athletes."
Page's triumph was short-lived. His teammates piled on Page during a
practice drill, breaking his neck; he was paralyzed and died thirty-eight
days later.[52]

The success of the Alabama Crimson Tide in 1961—eleven consecu-
tive victories and a 10–3 win over Arkansas in the Sugar Bowl—took place
against the backdrop of the civil rights movement, especially the violent

clashes between segregationists and Freedom Riders in Anniston, Birmingham, and Montgomery, Alabama, during the summer of 1961. Not a few white Alabamians reckoned Alabama's success on the gridiron that fall as validation for the "Southern way of life," a euphemism for racial segregation, and they applauded the legendary Crimson Tide coach, Paul "Bear" Bryant, for holding the line against integration. "Your men stood like Stonewall Jackson," Frank Boykin, a member of Congress from Mobile, wrote to Bryant at season's end. "There was so much joy, there was so much pleasure that you gave all of the home folks and people all over the South and the people all over the Nation that want us to keep some part of our way of life." Employing once again the nomenclature of militarism, Boykin referred to the coach as "General Bear Bryant."[53]

Although Bryant was considered a racial moderate by the contemporary standards of the South, and he quietly brokered a deal that allowed Alabama to play racially integrated Penn State in the Liberty Bowl in 1959, he kept his teams white. His intransigent stand against integration cost him a trip to the Rose Bowl in 1961, a bid he coveted. "I would just about walk out there for a chance to play in it," Bryant conceded, "and I believe my players would too." He even sent word that he had no objections to playing against the integrated UCLA team. The Rose Bowl Committee, bowing to pressure from southern Californians newly attuned to racial injustice and violence in the South, refused to extend a bid to the nation's number one–ranked team.[54]

Even after George C. Wallace's histrionic "stand in the schoolhouse door" in Tuscaloosa on June 11, 1963, Bryant refused to integrate the Crimson Tide, although the University of Alabama had begun admitting African Americans. The 1965 team was voted national champion for the third time in five years—the last all-white squad so honored—but the Crimson Tide finished third in the voting the following year, despite another undefeated season. Many observers, including some outside of the South, interpreted the snub as retaliation for the killing of four little girls at the Sixteenth Street Baptist Church, for the Bloody Sunday confrontation at the foot of the Edmund Pettus Bridge, for Bull Connor's police dogs and fire hoses unleashed on nonviolent demonstrators in Birmingham's Kelly Ingram Park. Following the release of the 1966 poll, Theophilus Eugene "Bull" Connor sent Bryant a letter of condolence.

"Thousands of others in this State and country know that Alabama is Number 1," the commissioner wrote.[55]

Bryant, stung by the poll, extended an olive branch, albeit one wrapped in both understatement and exaggerated deference. "A few years ago, we had segregation problems," he announced. "But now, we'd like to ask the help of you fellows up above us in the North, who have been our critics, to help us get games with the Big Ten, the Big Eight, the Pacific Coast." Alabama players followed their coach's lead by displaying Southern chivalry toward the University of Nebraska's Black players—helping opponents to their feet after knocking them down—even as the Crimson Tide dispatched the Cornhuskers 34–7 in the 1967 Sugar Bowl.[56]

Toward the end of the 1960s, Bryant moved slowly, cautiously toward the integration of his football team. In 1967, he invited Black high school coaches to his summer coaching clinic in Tuscaloosa, although he also assured the university's president that he would not sign African American athletes anytime soon. "We have not actively attempted to recruit any colored athletes in the State because we have none that we felt qualified both academically and athletically," he said. By 1969, however, with his own program in decline, and with six of the ten Southeast Conference teams having signed Black players, Bryant needed fresh talent. Wilbur Jackson, of Ozark, Alabama, became the first African American recruit to the Alabama football team in 1970, the same year that Reubin Askew of Florida, Dale Bumpers of Arkansas, and Jimmy Carter of Georgia were elected governors of their respective states and emerged as the face of the New South.[57]

More important for Bryant was the Crimson Tide's home opener on September 12, 1970, when the all-white Alabama varsity team hosted the University of Southern California at Legion Field in Birmingham. (Jackson did not play because NCAA rules at the time did not allow freshmen to play on the varsity team.) A pair of African American running backs for USC perforated the Crimson Tide defense on their way to a 42–21 win: Clarence Davis, who grew up in Birmingham dreaming of playing for Alabama, and Sam "Bam" Cunningham, who rushed that day for 212 yards. "I want some guys who can play like those players," Bryant said after the game. "I don't care what color they are." The following fall, Wilbur Jackson and John Mitchell, a junior college transfer, became the first

African Americans to play for the Crimson Tide varsity, and two years later one-third of Alabama's starting lineup was Black. Bryant remarked years later that "Sam Cunningham did more for integration in Alabama in 60 minutes than Martin Luther King Jr. did in 20 years."[58]

For Bryant, integration worked. The University of Alabama rebounded from its late-1960s slump to compile a record of 116–15–1 in the seventies, including three national titles and eight SEC championships between 1971 and 1981. *Time* magazine, which had criticized Bryant as a martinet in 1961, placed him on its September 29, 1980, cover with the title SUPERCOACH emblazoned over his signature houndstooth fedora.[59]

The tide of racial integration had finally washed over college football in the Old South; the sport surmounted the race barrier. The career of Paul "Bear" Bryant uncannily tracked that of his fellow Alabamian, George C. Wallace. Bryant fielded his first Crimson Tide team in 1958, the same year Wallace ran unsuccessfully for governor as a racial moderate. Vowing never to be "outni**ered" again, Wallace followed the course of racial demagoguery to the governor's mansion, famously declaring in his 1963 inaugural address, "Segregation now, segregation tomorrow, segregation forever."[60]

Bryant's approach to integration was cautious and tepid. As Wallace dispatched Alabama state troopers to the Edmund Pettus Bridge with orders to stop the march from Selma to Montgomery, Bryant considered inviting Black coaches to his coaching clinic in Tuscaloosa. As Wallace was gearing up for his "states' rights" campaign for the presidency, Bryant instructed his players to comport themselves as Southern gentlemen in their Sugar Bowl game against the integrated University of Nebraska team.

Yet, just as sports fans like to conjecture about counterfactual scenarios—what if the referee hadn't called pass interference, or suppose the running back hadn't fumbled on third-and-goal—it's tempting to speculate about how the history of Alabama, or the South in general, might have unfolded differently if Bryant had taken an earlier, more courageous stand for racial integration. The Crimson Tide coach had risen to the status of demigod by the mid-1960s. His would have been a powerful voice in a racially troubled time.

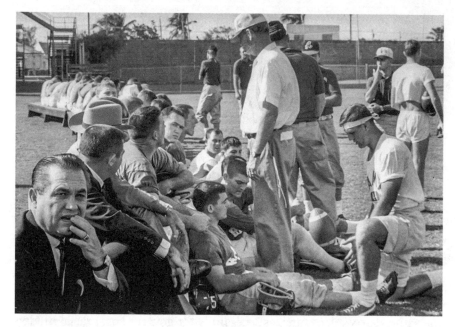

George C. Wallace (1919–1998), governor of Alabama, left foreground, visits Alabama football practice in advance of the 1965 Orange Bowl game. Paul "Bear" Bryant (1913–1983) is standing at center. The University of Alabama Libraries Special Collections.

Integration in football may have come earlier than in other sports, but it was not always smooth. The line between honest competition and racial targeting is always difficult to define in any sport, but it's especially challenging in a sport where violence is embedded in the game itself. When a crushing tackle broke Matthew Bullock's collarbone in a 1903 Ivy League game, a Princeton player acknowledged that the blow was meant to remove the Dartmouth receiver from the game—not, he insisted, because Bullock was Black, but because he was the best player on the field. In 1923, Jack Trice, the first African American athlete at Iowa State University, suffered fatal injuries during his first football game, against the University of Minnesota at Northrop Field in Minneapolis.[61]

Sometimes the attacks were blatant. By the time Johnny Bright and his Drake University teammates took the field to play Oklahoma A&M College (now Oklahoma State University) in Stillwater on October 20, 1951, the home team was gunning for the Bulldogs' star quarterback, who had broken the NCAA's career rushing record the previous year and was a favorite for the Heisman Trophy, college football's highest honor. His 266.7 average yards per game as an individual in 1950 exceeded that of thirty-nine major college teams. All week during practice leading up to the Stillwater game, the Oklahoma A&M coach had enjoined his players to "get that ni**er." Both the local newspaper and the student newspaper reported in the days leading up to the game that Bright was a marked man, and it was an open secret on the Stillwater campus that Bright would not be around by the end of the game. Three times in the opening seven minutes, Wilbanks Smith, an Oklahoma A&M lineman and team captain, crashed his forearm into Bright's face—well after the quarterback had handed off the ball and was observing the play. The third hit shattered Bright's jaw. The *Tulsa Daily World* reported that Smith "hit Bright with such force that both his feet were off the ground." A sequence of photographs published the following day in the *Des Moines Sunday Register* under the headline "Bright's Jaw Broken" established both the intent and the effects of the blow. "You never hit a person that many times unless you do it on purpose," Bright said. Piling insult on top of injury, a ticket agent at the Stillwater railroad station refused to allow the injured Bright to sit with his white teammates on the ride home to Des Moines.[62]

African American players suffered taunts and gratuitous violence, especially in the early years of desegregation, and when they sought to band together in solidarity, their efforts were often frustrated by authorities. In 1969, for example, in the face of racial tensions across the nation, fourteen Black players on the University of Wyoming football team proposed to wear black armbands in their game against Brigham Young University. They claimed they had been targeted for abuse by BYU players when the teams faced off the previous year, and they also wanted to protest the Latter-day Saints' continued exclusion of Black men from the Mormon priesthood (the ban was finally lifted in 1978). When the players approached their coach, Lloyd Eaton, with their armband proposal, however, he summarily dismissed all fourteen players from the team.[63]

Football surmounted the three Rs—region, religion, and race—on its way to near universal approbation in North America, but it has faced another challenge since its origins. As befits a game that replicates the stratagems of war, violence is endemic to football. Just as violence on the battlefield produces casualties, so too the violence of football breeds injuries, thereby generating controversy surrounding the game that persists to this day. "There will be injuries," Walter Camp acknowledged, "but we should minimize these as far as possible, and every effort toward this end will be made." Elsewhere, he shrugged off such concerns, noting that "there are worse things in a college life than a sprained ankle, a twisted knee, or even a broken nose." A college president defended the virtues of football, even as he conceded its liabilities: "It breaks collar-bones, gouges out eyes, sprains ankles." The medical director of the School for Physical Education at Harvard catalogued common injuries: "sprains, cuts, bruises, fractures, and dislocations of various parts of the body and limbs, and concussion of the brain."[64]

From the earliest days of the game, spectators and players reveled in the game's violence. Commenting on the Bloody Monday football game between freshmen and sophomores at Harvard, John Langdon Sibley noted in his diary that "the object of each class is to kick the others & 'bark their shins' as much as possible." When calling for an end to football on campus, *Harvard Magazine* cited "the brutality of the game." The *New York Daily Tribune* attributed the football mania at Yale to an impulse to "dislocate somebody's anatomy." When football arrived in Ackley, Iowa, in 1874, the *Ackley Independent* noted that "loving mothers and kind hearted sisters are looking up poultice recipes just now; preparing for the bruised shins and stubbed toes that are the 'thorns among the roses' in the foot-ball game." And the *Daily Kennebec Journal* in Maine reported that "little boys in the Saco schools receive so many injuries from rough games, football, etc., that the parents are endeavoring to have the superintendent put a stop to the rough sport."[65]

Violence in football extended beyond the playground to the collegiate gridiron. The 1877 championship game between Yale and Princeton, played on the St. George Cricket Grounds in Hoboken, New Jersey, produced "bloody noses and severe bruises"—and a tie. One Harvard player described the 1878 contest with Princeton "the roughest ever played" and declared "the Princeton boys are the toughest we ever met." Contemporary accounts told of bloodied bodies, broken and amputated limbs, and displaced dentition. The *New York Record* judged that in the Princeton-Yale game of 1884, "more bodily harm was done than it would be possible to accomplish in a score of boxing exhibitions at Madison Square Garden." Word of football's brutality even extended across the Atlantic. A Munich newspaper described the 1894 Yale-Harvard game as "awful butchery," noting that seven players "were so severely injured that they had to be carried from the field in a dying condition." The *Münchener Nachtrichten* tallied the casualties: "One player had his back broken, another lost an eye, and a third lost a leg." The *New York Times* covered the same game, which took place before a crowd of twenty-five thousand on a crystalline November day in Springfield, Massachusetts. "An ordinary rebellion in the South American or Central American States is as child's play compared with the destructiveness of a day's game," the paper said, "and the record of French duels for the last dozen years fails to show such a list of casualties as this one game of football produced." The newspaper reported that "Charles Brewer of the Harvard team had his leg broken, Wrighting-ton had a collarbone broken, and Hallowell goes back to Cambridge with a broken nose." As for Yale, two players "were seriously injured about the head," and other players sustained injuries "that would land any one but a football player in a hospital for repairs." The *Times* refuted rumors that a lineman for Yale had died at the Springfield hospital.[66]

When asked about collegiate football, John L. Sullivan, heavyweight champion boxer, remarked, "There's murder in that game."[67]

After the turn of the century, football injuries mounted as the game became more popular. The *Journal of the American Medical Association* counted twelve deaths from football in 1902. At the end of 1905, the *Chicago Tribune* reported on the casualties of the football season just past, which the newspaper characterized as a "death harvest": 159 serious injuries and 19 fatalities. When Harvard's football coach, Bill Reid, arrived for practice on Thursday afternoon, October 12, 1905, the team doctor presented him with the daily injury list. Twenty-one players were sidelined, with injuries ranging from a sprained back and injured wrist to dislocated elbow and fractured zygoma; during that afternoon's practice, another player broke his collarbone.[68]

Such carnage caught the attention of even the president, Theodore Roosevelt, whose asthma had prevented him from playing football at Harvard but who nevertheless remained a fan, hailing football as "the greatest exercise of fine moral qualities, such as resolution, courage, endurance and capacity to hold one's own and stand up under punishment." Roosevelt had professed indifference to the violence of football. "I do not feel any particular sympathy for the person who gets battered about a good deal," he declared in 1903, "so long as it is not fatal."[69]

By 1905, however, with the number of fatalities increasing, some voices called for reform. Charles W. Eliot, president of Harvard, had long opposed football because of its brutality. "The game of foot-ball grows worse and worse as regards foul and violent play, and the number and gravity of injuries which the players suffer," he wrote in his annual report. "It has become perfectly clear that the game as now played is unfit for college use." Shailer Mathews, professor at the University of Chicago Divinity School, acknowledged that football "teaches virility and courage," but "so does war." He urged the invention of a new game, one that would "not require the services of a physician, the maintenance of a hospital, and the celebration of funerals." On December 8, 1905, representatives of thirteen colleges met at the Murray Hill Hotel in Manhattan to discuss a resolution "that the game of football, as played under existing rules should be abolished." Five schools, including Columbia, supported the resolution.[70]

After Roosevelt's own son, Ted, sustained several injuries while playing on the Harvard freshman team, the president summoned representatives from Princeton, Yale, and Harvard to the White House. Even the secretary of state, Elihu Root, was in attendance. "I demand that football change its rules or be abolished," Roosevelt bellowed. "Change the game or forsake it!" The officials agreed to review "the rules of the game of foot ball relating to roughness, holding and foul play"; toward that end, they formed the Intercollegiate Athletic Association. Subsequent alterations to the rules, including outlawing the flying wedge and allowing the forward pass, made the game marginally safer, although casualties rose again in 1909: two fatalities, and the Navy quarterback was paralyzed in a game against Villanova.[71]

Violence, however, accounts for the much of the appeal of football, then and now. "It's the violence of the sport," Hall of Fame quarterback Troy Aikman said. "The violence of the sport attracts us to the game." By any measure, the United States is a violent society, an observation confirmed in the daily newspaper and the nightly news with horrific stories about gun violence and attacks against children. Consider the unspeakable violence of slavery and the violence directed against women and against ethnic and racial minorities. The emergence of the game of football coincided with the nineteenth-century push into the West beneath the banner of Manifest Destiny, the Civil War, and the Spanish-American War. The military goal was annihilation of the adversary by means of violence. The earliest football games reflected that ethic. The big three powerhouses—Princeton, Yale, and Harvard—routinely destroyed their opponents on the gridiron. Between 1883 and 1892, for example, Yale played 112 games, losing only three and tying two; one hundred of those games were shutouts. In 1888, Yale outscored its opponents 698 to 0. In 1890, Princeton beat four opponents: 50–0, 60–0, 115–0, and 85–0. In 1887, Harvard outscored its opponents 660–23.[72]

Given such a close connection between combat and football, it is no coincidence that as the tactics of warfare have changed on the battlefield, so have gridiron strategies. In the early days of football, just as in military confrontations from the Civil War through World War I, skirmishes took place almost solely on the ground, what became known in World War I as trench warfare. Although the forward pass was legalized in 1905, it only gradually took hold (in part because early rules mandated that an incomplete pass incurred a fifteen-yard penalty and a pass that fell to the ground untouched would cede the ball to the opposing team). The forward pass was adopted by Glenn Scobey "Pop" Warner, son of a cavalry officer in the Civil War, and his Carlisle Industrial School football team (the "Indians") in 1907—and to great effect. Eventually the forward pass was picked up by other teams, including the University of Notre Dame, and gradually the "aerial attack" on the gridiron gained favor, roughly at the same time that the strategies of warfare changed with bombing missions in World War II, the Korean War, and the Vietnam War. In language eerily reminiscent of military tactics in Vietnam, a 1967 documentary about the NFL, *They Call It Pro Football*, described linebackers as "search-and-destroy men of the defense." As for offensive strategies, according to statistics for the National Football League, the number of passing plays surpassed running plays about the year 1980. In the 1940s,

NFL teams passed for an average 144 yards a game; in the 2010 decade, the average was 234 yards a game. Drew Brees, quarterback of the New Orleans Saints, passed for 46,770 yards in the 2010s; Sammy Baugh, by contrast, the decade leader of the 1940s, passed for 17,002 yards.[73]

That correlation and the adaptation of football to changing circumstances should not be surprising. Whereas baseball rejects the horological icon of industrialism, clings to sylvan values, and was slow to embrace new technologies such as video review, football perpetually reinvents itself, nimbly seizing on the latest innovations, from strategies and in-game communications to training and equipment (which advocates insist has increased the safety of the game).

Football, evolved from ancient games, reflects both martial values of combat and modern values of innovation. It has never lacked for critics over the decades, but football has endured. By some metrics, it is more popular than ever. "Leave the game to its natural course," Eugene L. Richards, captain of the football team at Yale and grandson of a general in the Revolutionary War, argued in 1886, "and foot-ball will work out its own salvation."[74]

CHAPTER 3

Soul of a Nation

The Canadian Confederation and the Origins of Hockey

What is the national game of Canada to be—
Cricket, Lacrosse, or Base Ball?

—GOLDWIN SMITH

Some people say hockey is like religion, but that's wrong. Hockey
is like faith. Religion is something between you and other people;
it's full of interpretations and theories and opinions. But faith . . .
that's just between you and God. It's what you feel in your chest
when the referee glides out to the center circle between two players,
when you hear the sticks strike each other and see the black disk
fall between them. Then it's just between you and hockey.

—FREDRIK BACKMAN

"Canadian sports," W. George Beers noted in 1883, "have a character of
their own. They smack more of the ungoverned and ungovernable than
the games of the Old World, and seem to resent the impost of regulations." I cannot imagine a better description of the game of hockey, a
quintessentially Canadian game and one inextricably tied to winter. "In
the towns of the Canadian north country," Leslie McFarlane wrote in
1935, "hockey is more than a game; it is almost a religion."[1]

The roots of hockey extend well back into the history of what is now
the British Isles; games called "shinty" and "hurling" are antecedents.

Hurling, of Gaelic and Irish origins and very possibly the world's oldest field game, is played with a stick, or *hurley*, a wooden, axe-shaped paddle which is curved outward at the end. The object, as with field hockey, is either to shoot a small ball, called a *sliotar*, over the crossbar between the goalposts (similar to a field goal in American football) for one point, or below the crossbar, past the goalkeeper, and into the net, for three points. Players, fifteen to a side, can scoop up the ball with their sticks, catch the ball with their hands, slap the ball with an open hand, or strike the ball, similar to cricket or baseball; they can carry the ball in their hands for no more than four steps, and skilled players can balance the ball on the end of their sticks while advancing the ball toward the opponent's goal. The women's version of hurling is called *camogie*.

Shinty, also known as *camanchd* or *iomain* in Gaelic, derives from prehistoric Scotland and is now played principally in the Scottish Highlands. It is a fast-paced game similar to both lacrosse and field hockey. Players, twelve to a team, use a curved stick, called a *caman*, to advance the ball, which was originally wood or bone and now is leather; players can play the ball in the air and may also kick or stop the ball with their feet, although only the goalkeeper is allowed to use his hands.

Hockey, then, evolved from several sources, including hurley and shinty, which became "shinny" in North America. The genealogy of ice hockey also extends back to field hockey in England, but its immediate ancestor is the First Nations game known as "baggataway" among the Algonquin and *tewaarathon* by the Iroquois Nation. One tradition surrounding the game holds that Jean de Brébeuf, French Jesuit missionary and martyr, thought that the stick used to play the game resembled a bishop's crozier, or cross, so the French dubbed it "lacrosse," although it is more likely that the derivation is from *jouer à la cross*, a term used back in France to describe games played with a curved stick.[2]

W. George Beers, who began playing the game at age six, watched the matches between Indians—the Akwesasne of Saint-Régis and the Iroquois of Caughnawaga—in the Montréal area, intently studying the game. Although he found much to admire both in the game and in the skill of the players, he believed that the game needed to be rationalized. Contemporary accounts of lacrosse played by the First Nations told of no boundaries to the playing field and as many as thousands of players on

Caughnawaga lacrosse team, with W. George Beers and Henry Beckett, ca. 1867.
McCord Museum, Montréal, M930.50.1.742.

either side—the very definition of "mob game"—though that number is likely exaggerated. Beers, reared a Presbyterian, believed that some regulations were required if lacrosse were to flourish (the catchphrase for Presbyterians is that everything must be done "decently and in order").[3]

By 1860, the same year Beers played goaltender for the Montréal Lacrosse Club, he codified and published a rule book that specified field size, the number of players, and the distance between goals. Lacrosse became increasingly popular among whites, and in Kingston, Ontario, on September 26, 1867, Beers and other boosters from Québec and Ontario formed the National Lacrosse Association, consisting of twenty-nine clubs, and he aspired to christen lacrosse as "Our National Field Game." Two years later, Beers published *Lacrosse: The National Game of Canada*, which set out "to extend a knowledge of the game of Lacrosse, to systematize its principles and practice, and to perpetuate it as the National game of Canada."[4]

For Beers and other Canadians in the 1860s, national identity was very much at stake. Following the Union victory in the Civil War, the United States boasted a strong army, and some American newspapers talked about annexing Canada, in part as retribution against Great Britain for supporting the Confederacy. Canadians were not particularly enthusiastic about that idea, and the possible threat from the south, exacerbated by rumors that the United States would purchase Alaska from Russia, had the effect of energizing talks about a Canadian confederation, which had been under discussion since 1839. Negotiations among colonial politicians began anew in 1864, and in 1867 the British Parliament passed the British North America Act, which created the Dominion of Canada, consisting of Ontario, New Brunswick, Nova Scotia, and Québec.

The new nation needed an identity, one separate from Britain, and Beers believed that sports would help to forge that identity. Whereas cricket had been the game of British imperialism, lacrosse would epitomize Canadian nationalism. "Whatever tends to cultivate this nationality is no frivolous influence," he wrote, "even should it be a boyish sport." Beers had imbibed the ideals of Muscular Christianity from England, and he argued that sport was essential to the Canadian character. But he was no Anglophile. In a letter published in the *Montréal Daily News* in April 1867, Beers pushed hard for Canadians to forsake cricket, which he regarded as sissifying, in favor of lacrosse, because it ran counter to England's bourgeois sensibilities, which saw sports as refined, a breeding ground for gentility. Beers believed that lacrosse was aggressive, brutal, and rugged, and those characteristics mimicked the rough-and-tumble Canadian landscape and character. "While not advocating pugnacity," he wrote, "men—and women, too—admire manly youth; and if our National game, while exercising the manly virtues, also trains the national and the moral, it will, undoubtedly, help to make us better men; and genuine 'pluck' will never go out of fashion in Canada."[5]

Lest anyone miss the point, Beers made the argument explicit. "As cricket, wherever played by Britons, is a link of loyalty to bind them to their home so may lacrosse be to Canadians," Beers wrote in 1867, the year of Canada's confederation. "We may yet find it will do as much for our young Dominion as the Olympian games did for Greece or cricket for our Motherland." If Greece was shaped by the Olympic Games and

W. George Beers (1841–1900), a student of lacrosse and a Montréal dentist, argued at the time of the Canadian Confederation that Canadians needed their own game, lacrosse, which was more appropriate to the Canadian character than cricket. McCord Museum, Montréal, I-9223.1.

Emblem of the National Lacrosse Association, asserting that lacrosse (not cricket) was the game that reflected the values of the new confederation. McCord Museum, Montréal, M930.50.1.742.

Britain by cricket, the character of Canada, Beers argued, would derive from lacrosse. The Montréal Lacrosse Club unofficially declared lacrosse Canada's national game at the time of confederation; tragically and paradoxically, various lacrosse organizations limited the participation of Indigenous players that same year and barred them outright in 1880.[6]

Anglo-Canadian cultural imperialism and colonialism elbowed aside First Nations people, those who had been playing the game for centuries. Beers declared that his domestication of the game heralded a "new era" for the sport. "When civilization tamed the manners and habits of the Indian," he wrote, "it reflected its modifying influence upon his amusements, and thus was Lacrosse gradually divested of its radical rudeness and brought-to a more sober sport." The motto of the National Lacrosse Association, formed the same year as confederation, was "Our Country and Our Game," and by 1887 the *Chicago Daily Tribune* noted, "Lacrosse is to the Canadian what base-ball is to the Yankee and cricket to the Englishmen."[7]

The evolution of lacrosse into ice hockey in North America remains a matter of considerable dispute, so much so that an organization called the Society for International Hockey Research has taken upon itself the task of both cataloguing and adjudicating various competing claims. The society begins by establishing its definition of hockey: "a game played on an ice rink in which two opposing teams of skaters, using curved sticks, try to drive a small disc, ball or block into or through the opposite goals."[8]

If there is any town east of, say, Toronto that does *not* claim to be the birthplace of hockey, I should like to know about it. J. W. "Bill" Fitsell, the game's premier historian, believes that the most likely candidates are Kingston, Montréal, and Halifax, although some historians place the first game in 1839 on Chippewa Creek (Niagara Falls, Ontario), others make a case for Windsor or Pictou, Nova Scotia, and even newer evidence points back to England. The remote outpost of Délįne, on the shores of Great Bear Lake in the Northwest Territories, lays claim to the naissance of ice hockey on the basis of a diary entry from 1825, and there is some credibility to the claim that the first ice hockey was played on Christmas Day, 1812, along the Red River near Pembina, North Dakota.[9]

Kingston, once the capital of the United Province of Canada, staked its claim in a hockey program in 1933: "From the time the first game of hockey in the world was played on the harbour ice, Kingston has been noted as the real home of the sport." A diary entry from Arthur Henry Freeling, dated January 24, 1843, reads, "Began to skate this year, improved quickly and had great fun at hockey on the ice." In another scenario, ice hockey began when members of the Royal Canadian Rifles swatted a lacrosse ball on the harbor ice on Christmas Day, 1855, a claim that has since been discredited because meteorological evidence has established that the harbor was not frozen on that day.[10]

Partisans of Halifax-Dartmouth note a plethora of references, dated as early as 1827, to "ricket" and "hurley" played on the frozen lakes in the area. "Hockey ought to be sternly forbidden, as it is not only annoying but dangerous," an article in the January 25, 1864, *Halifax Morning Sun* cautioned. "In its right place, hockey is a noble game, and deserving of every encouragement, but on the ice it is in its wrong place, and should be prohibited." Those who assert the primacy of Halifax-Dartmouth also point to a newspaper article in the *Halifax Evening Reporter*, published February 19, 1867, which demonstrates that hockey was played on Oathill Lake, in Dartmouth, outside of Halifax. There, soldiers from nearby military bases and naval ports engaged in "a match game called hockey," played on skates with sticks. The article noted "many sore shins" but "not a head was broke." Because the hockey game took place concurrently with other activities on the ice, the writer cautioned that "if exclusive games of hockey are to be played, a crowded lake is no place for it."[11]

If the term "organized" is added to the formula, most hockey origin narratives converge on Montréal in the 1870s, a city whose population had recently swollen above one hundred thousand. Montréal saw a burst of building and expansion during that decade—hotels, churches, schools, and office buildings—as the city became Canada's largest industrial center. The Montréal Stock Exchange was established in 1874, the same year as Mount Royal Park, designed by Frederick Law Olmsted. Train service to New York City opened the following year. The University of Montréal was founded in 1878, and the French-Canadian industrialist J. A. I. Craig introduced electric streetlamps in 1879.

James George Aylwin Creighton, a native of Halifax and an alumnus of Dalhousie University, made his way to Montréal in 1872. An employee of the Lachine Canal Company, Creighton had a varied career as journalist, engineer, attorney, and athlete. In the mid-1870s, he served as judge of figure skating at the Victoria Skating Rink, located at the corner of Stanley and Drummond Streets. The rink, the exterior of which a British journalist likened to a Methodist chapel, had been constructed in 1862 by a group of elite Montréalers, all of them Anglo-Canadians. Having witnessed earlier iterations of hockey in Nova Scotia, Creighton organized a Wednesday evening game, nine players to a team, for his McGill University friends at the Victoria Skating Rink on March 3, 1875.[12]

The following day, the *Montréal Gazette* compared the game to lacrosse and shinty, and the *Montréal Star* reported that the participants "excited much merriment as they wheeled and dodged each other." The *Montréal Daily Witness* also ran an account of the game, noting that a flat piece of board was used instead of a ball; it "slid about between the players with great velocity." The paper also noted an "unfortunate disagreement" leading to a fight in which "a bench was broken and other damage caused." Another report appeared two days later in the *Ottawa Times* and the *Kingston Daily British Whig*, an account that focused on violence. "A disgraceful sight took place in Montreal at the Victoria Skating Rink over a game of hockey," the article read. "Shins and heads were battered, benches smashed, and the lady spectators fled in confusion."[13]

Because the game was played within a confined space—the Victoria Skating Rink's ice surface measured eighty-five by two hundred feet—players eventually adopted a disc instead of a ball, making hockey the only team sport not to use a ball (the term "puck" derived from "free poke," or shot, in Irish hurling). By 1877 the first set of rules—seven in all—was published, an adaptation of the field hockey rules produced in England two years earlier. Unlike basketball, whose origins can be traced to a single source at a specific time and place, it was clear even in the early years of the game that hockey had evolved over time and likely from multiple sources. As Emanuel M. Orlick, director of physical education at McGill, noted, "Hockey was no brainchild conceived in the night and put into practice the next day."[14]

Creighton made no claim to being the father of ice hockey, but McGill's Orlick credited the Victoria match in 1875 with exciting popular interest in hockey, leading to the formation of various teams. Two years after the first game, Creighton became captain of the first hockey club in Canada, and a hockey tournament was organized in conjunction with the Montréal Winter Carnival beginning in 1883. An adjunct exhibition featuring teams from Montréal was held in Burlington, Vermont, in 1886, as part of the Burlington Carnival of Winter Sports, marking the first international hockey game. So novel was the game that the *Burlington Free Press* felt obliged to explain it. "For the benefit of those who have never seen the game played," the newspaper said, "it should be stated that it bears a striking resemblance to polo, the ball instead of being round is round one way and flat the other, like a boys' cartwheel sawed out of a board." That same year, 1886, new rules governing hockey—now increased to sixteen—were published by the Amateur Hockey Association of Canada.[15]

Following its debut in Montréal, hockey spread quickly to other cities. A McGill alumnus brought hockey to Kingston in 1879. Two Ottawa men witnessed hockey at the Montréal Winter Carnival in 1883; within two months they had organized a hockey club in the nation's capital. Creighton himself, having earned a law degree from McGill, left Montréal for Ottawa in 1882, where he embarked on a long and prestigious career as law clerk of the Senate and introduced parliamentary and government officials to hockey. Creighton played on various teams, including the Ottawa Rebels and the Rideau Club, until age forty.[16]

Whereas Montréal was Francophone in the nineteenth century, Toronto was decidedly British, with vestiges of Puritanism. In 1845, the Ontario legislature had passed the Upper Canada Lord's Day Act, which forbade the playing of sports on Sunday, although the legislation was enforced only episodically. In the 1886 civic election, voters elected William Holmes Howland as mayor, the moral-reform candidate, with a mandate to restrict commercial and recreational activities on Sunday in what was by then known as the City of Churches. Founded two years later, the Lord's Day Alliance, a federation consisting predominantly of Presbyterians and Methodists, sought to enforce the prohibition against the playing of sports on Sunday; because of weekday work schedules, this had the effect of denying organized team sports to the lower, working classes.[17]

Despite these limitations, Toronto was emerging as a sports town. Private sporting clubs—cricket, cycling, golf, rowing, curling, sailing, and lacrosse—proliferated. The Central YMCA was constructed in 1887, and the Toronto Athletic Club was formed in 1892, the same year a new gymnasium and fieldhouse opened at the University of Toronto. Lacrosse, still considered Canada's national game, was popular, and members of Toronto's lacrosse teams became local heroes as they perennially contended for national championships.[18]

Torontonians were well aware of hockey, having read newspaper accounts of games in Montréal, including the hockey tournament in conjunction with the Montréal Winter Carnival. In November 1886, the Toronto Lacrosse Club announced that it was forming a hockey club so that lacrosse players could maintain their physical conditioning through the winter. Other sporting clubs, including the Wanderers Bicycle Club and the Toronto Athletics Lacrosse Club, followed suit, and the first game took place on January 16, 1888, at the Caledonia Rink. Hockey soon caught on in Toronto, and when news arrived two years later that the Rideau Hall Rebels of Ottawa were coming to take on Toronto's finest, the city was abuzz with excitement, especially because the Ottawa team included several members of Parliament and two sons of Canada's governor general, Frederick Arthur Stanley, better known as Lord Stanley. Still, the *Toronto Globe* felt obliged to explain to its readers that hockey "is somewhat like lacrosse, but quicker."[19]

On November 27, 1890, meeting at the Queen's Hotel in Toronto, more than a dozen delegates from Kingston, Ottawa, Bowmanville, Lindsay, Hamilton, and Toronto formed the Ontario Hockey Association. The following year, Toronto bankers and financiers followed Montréal's lead and established the Bank League of Toronto. By the turn of the twentieth century, teams and leagues were booming in Toronto as hockey captured the city's imagination. "For dash, vigour, skill and brilliancy," the *Toronto Mail* declared, "there is possibly not its equal anywhere in the world."[20]

By 1899 Arthur Farrell published *Hockey: Canada's Royal Winter Game*. He described hockey as "fast, furious, brilliant" and called it "our most popular winter sport." He christened it "the game of games" and declared it "the most fascinating, the most exciting, the most scientific." Indeed, on the cusp of the twentieth century, hockey was emerging as Canada's game, one that, like the nation itself, combined the raw intensity of the frozen wilderness with the latest in technological advances, especially in the design of skates. "It is safe to say that hockey had definitely taken its place among the national sports of Canada," wrote Canadian novelist J. Macdonald Oxley.[21]

Americans also took notice. St. Paul's School in Concord, New Hampshire, claims to be the "cradle of American hockey." One of the school's masters, James P. Conover, had visited Montréal. "I got sticks, pucks (wooden tubes covered with leather) and rules from Canada myself," he recalled. On the afternoon of November 17, 1883, students gathered at the Lower School Pond to witness the first hockey game played by Americans in the United States.[22]

In 1908, the school's best athlete, Hobart Amory Hare "Hobey" Baker, took up the game. "He is the wonder player of hockey," the *Boston Journal*

Rink on Lower School Pond, St. Paul's School, Concord, New Hampshire, 1911.
The school claims that the first hockey game in the United States was played
here on November 17, 1883. Ohrstrom Library, St. Paul's School.

wrote, "without a doubt the greatest amateur hockey player ever developed in this country or Canada." When Baker played in Montréal, Canadians initially were dubious—until they witnessed his play. "Uncle Sam has had the cheek to develop a firstclass hockey player," the *Montréal Press* conceded. "We had always smiled a cynical grin at the thought. A few minutes of Baker on the ice convinced the most skeptical." *Sports Illustrated* called him "the golden boy of American sport."[23]

Hobey Baker enrolled at Princeton University, where he was named captain of both the hockey and the football teams. Known for his sportsmanship and clean play—he visited the opponents' locker room after every game to shake hands with the players—Baker, who perished in a plane crash at the conclusion of World War I, was among the charter class inducted into the Hockey Hall of Fame in 1945 and among the initial four athletes commemorated in the Sports Bay and Chapel in the Cathedral of St. John the Divine in New York City. Princeton's hockey arena is the Hobey Baker Memorial Rink.[24]

At a dinner honoring the Ottawa Hockey Club, on March 18, 1892, the governor-general's assistant announced that Frederick Arthur Stanley had commissioned a "Dominion Hockey Challenge Cup" for the best amateur hockey team. When the cup arrived from London the following year, the *Ottawa Journal* promptly dubbed it the Stanley Cup. The Montréal AAAs won the first championship in 1893, and competition for the cup had the effect of nationalizing—even internationalizing—the game in the 1890s, as hockey spread to the Maritimes, to New England, and to western Canada. Students at Yale University began to play hockey in 1893 (a decade after the St. Paul's game). Clubs from Winnipeg, Manitoba, won the Stanley Cup in 1896 and 1901.[25]

Although the founders of the Amateur Hockey Association of Canada vowed to protect the game from professionalism, the growing popularity of the sport at the turn of the twentieth century made it increasingly difficult. Sporting clubs and university alumni were taking up the game, and the construction of covered arenas insulated participants from the vicissitudes of the weather. These new venues accommodated spectators, who in turn were lured not merely by word of mouth but by advances in communications and by coverage in the sports sections of newspapers.[26]

Hockey was quickly becoming a spectator sport, one capable of generating revenue. As the quality of play improved, the competition for players increased. The Montréal Hockey Club provided gifts to its players, everything from fruit to diamond rings celebrating the team's winning the Stanley Cup in 1903. Teams in Ontario and Pennsylvania began offering jobs and other emoluments for skilled players.[27]

Although the Canadian teams sought, albeit with mixed success, to retain their amateur status, the impetus for professionalism came from the International Hockey League. Formed on November 5, 1904, the league's guiding force was Jack "Doc" Gibson, an Ontario native, graduate of the Detroit College of Medicine, a dentist and hockey player, who had relocated to Houghton, in the copper-mining region of the Upper Peninsula of Michigan. Houghton was booming, a town one player remembered as "a great Saturday night fun place for miners who prefer to patronize something other than art museums or the opera house." Houghton had built its own hockey arena, the Amphidrome, in 1902, and the International Hockey League, the first professional hockey league, included five teams—from Calumet, Houghton, and Sault Ste. Marie, Michigan; Sault Ste. Marie, Ontario; and Pittsburgh. The league

The Houghton Amphidrome, built in 1902 on Portage Lake in Houghton, Michigan, was the first building constructed specifically for hockey in the United States. The first game took place on December 29, 1902; the Portage Lake team defeated the University of Toronto 13–2. Michigan Technological University Archives and Copper Country Historical Collections.

was able to entice Canadian players with the promise of a minimum of fifteen to forty dollars a week, offers frequently bundled with day jobs in the community.[28]

Although the International Hockey League lasted only three years, it altered the status of hockey in Canada. The Stanley Cup became the prize for professional hockey clubs, while the Amateur Athletic Union of Canada solicited a donation for a new trophy, the Allan Cup, that would be awarded to amateurs.[29]

With the professionalism barrier leveled, a group of businessmen, led by J. Ambrose O'Brien, owner of a silver mine in Renfrew, Ontario, formed the National Hockey Association on December 2, 1909, with teams from Québec and Ontario. As befits a league founded by captains of industry and business, the owners sought to implement the latest and most efficient management techniques, including a salary cap. The days of players doubling as club administrators were numbered. The new league switched from two thirty-minute halves to three twenty-minute periods and dropped the number of players per side to six, thereby making the game faster and, not incidentally, reducing roster sizes from ten to eight. The *Toronto Daily Star* declared the owners' move "similar to the action of a big manufacturer in decreasing a working force."[30]

O'Brien, scion to a lumber and mining fortune, could afford to lure professional players to his Renfrew team, notably Frederick "Cyclone" Taylor and the Patrick brothers, Frank and Lester; the team became known as the Renfrew Millionaires. The NHA was winning the bidding war for skilled players. Soon, the Canadian Hockey Association asked for a merger.[31]

From its earliest days, the new league sought to mitigate ethnic differences. The founders of the National Hockey Association thought it important that French Canadians be involved, so they organized Les Canadiens de Montréal, a team owned by O'Brien but managed by Jack Laviolette. After a year, O'Brien transferred ownership to George Kennedy of Montréal with the understanding that the team would have no more than two non-Francophone players; in 1912, the league decided that the Canadiens would have exclusive rights to French Canadian players, who had become interested in the game through the influence of Irish Catholics in Québec colleges. Decades later, the dynastic success of the Canadiens from 1965 to 1979 (ten Stanley Cups) helped to inspire the ethnic pride that fueled Québec's Quiet Revolution.[32]

The National Hockey Association had won the bidding war for players against the Canada Hockey Association, but it soon faced another challenge from the west. Having decamped to British Columbia to help their father run his lumber business, Lester and Frank Patrick set up the Pacific Coast Hockey Association with the proceeds from the sale of the business in 1911. The Patrick brothers quickly constructed arenas in Vancouver and Victoria (both featuring artificial ice) and organized a league consisting of three teams. In advance of the 1912–13 season, the PCHA raided some of the best NHA players, including the Patricks' erstwhile teammate on the Renfrew Millionaires, Frederick "Cyclone" Taylor. The two leagues effected a rapprochement for the following season, which entailed honoring the other league's contracts and suspensions.

They also agreed that the Stanley Cup would be awarded to the winner of a championship series between the two leagues.[33]

When the PCHA, following the earlier precedent of the International Hockey League, expanded to Portland, Oregon, in 1914 and to Seattle the following year, professional hockey was now both international and represented on both sides of the continent. And to underscore that point, the Vancouver Millionaires won the Stanley Cup in 1915; the Seattle Metropolitans prevailed two years later.[34]

Back east, trouble was brewing within the National Hockey Association. In December 1914, league owners had persuaded Edward James "Eddie" Livingstone, a Toronto financier, to take over the Toronto Ontarios franchise. Livingstone, however, soon alienated his fellow owners because he believed that Toronto could support only one hockey team. He purchased the city's other team, the Blueshirts, and proceeded to consolidate the two into a single team. The owners objected because of the expense of traveling to Toronto for only one game and because the consolidation left the league with only five teams.

To exclude Livingstone, the owners voted to disband the National Hockey Association and then, days later, on November 22, 1917, they established the National Hockey League, adopting the same rules that had governed the defunct NHA. Frank Calder, secretary of the National Hockey Association, became president of the new National Hockey League, with "the understanding that there could be no appeal from his decisions."[35]

The NHL expanded in the 1920s, adding the Montréal Maroons and the Boston Bruins, the first team in the United States, in 1924. The New York Americans purchased the assets of the Hamilton Tigers in 1925, the same year the Pittsburgh Pirates came into the league. The New York Rangers were added in 1926, followed by the Chicago Black Hawks and the Detroit Red Wings, originally named the Cougars because the Detroit franchise had purchased the players of the defunct Victoria Cougars. The Toronto St. Patricks were sold and renamed the Maple Leafs in 1927.[36]

The Great Depression and the Second World War took a toll on the NHL. By the 1942–43 season the league was reduced to six teams, known as the "Original Six": Montréal Canadiens, Toronto Maple Leafs, Detroit Red Wings, Boston Bruins, Chicago Black Hawks, and the New York

Rangers. But by expanding to the United States, hockey was becoming more continental than strictly Canadian. In 1965, Al Purdy had written a poem entitled "Hockey Players," which read in part,

> For years a Canadian specific
> to salve the anguish of inferiority
> by being good at something the Americans aren't.

Beginning in the mid-1960s, however, the National Hockey League embarked on the first of several waves of expansion, which eventually brought hockey to such improbable venues as Los Angeles, Phoenix, Dallas, and Tampa Bay—far away from the backyard ponds of the frozen north.[37]

The professionalization of hockey in North America had the paradoxical effect of democratizing the game. As hockey became increasingly popular in the decades surrounding the turn of the twentieth century, the game initially played by elites in Montréal and Toronto gave way to more skilled players of any social class. The construction of more arenas provided additional ice time, but the proliferation of games on lakes and backyard ponds allowed more and more players to develop their skills, some of whom were able to parlay their prowess into professional contracts.[38]

The sensibilities of Muscular Christianity surrounded hockey as well. Black clergy in Nova Scotia formed the Colored Hockey League in 1895, an entity based on the Bible, the Baptist tradition, and the precepts of Booker T. Washington. Organizers believed that the game would be conducive to both spiritual formation and racial progress, cultivating the virtues of determination, discipline, and hard work.[39]

The influx of Irish and French-Canadian players—overwhelmingly Roman Catholic—around the turn of the twentieth century coincided with the addition of a religious fixture to the game: the penalty box. During hockey's early years, infractions on the ice were punished by monetary fines that referees would mete out to the offending players, like parking violations or traffic citations. By the early 1930s, after Francophone and Irish Catholics entered the game in greater numbers, penalty boxes were added, a riff on the Roman Catholic doctrine of penitence and absolution. Just as a parishioner enters the confessional, the hockey miscreant opens the door to the penalty box, what players call the "sin bin," to acknowledge and to atone for his transgression.[40]

Hockey's handling of deviance, usually fighting, replicates Christianity's approach to sin—that is, a combination of guilt and shame. Once a player is adjudged guilty, he serves his penance publicly; he is shamed in front of other players and in front of spectators. This approach combines Catholic and Protestant deterrents. The confessional is where guilt is acknowledged; the public nature of the punishment recalls the Puritan practice of shaming deviants by placing them in stocks on the village green.

The penalty box quickly became a fixture in hockey arenas. For decades, one box accommodated players from both teams, but a violent brawl between Toronto's Bob Pulford and Montréal's Terry Harper in 1963 prompted the construction of separate boxes, one for each team.

Other symbolism defines the hockey arena. The modern rink of professional hockey, with its rounded corners, replicates the backyard skating ponds so ubiquitous in Canada. Hockey legend Bobby Orr called backyard rinks "the heart and soul of hockey," and Wayne Gretzky, "the Great One," learned hockey in his backyard in Brantford, Ontario. *The Hockey Sweater*, a children's book written by Roch Carrier, recalling his childhood in Sainte-Justine, Québec, contains a sentiment once inscribed on the back of Canadian five-dollar bills: "The winters of my childhood were long, long seasons. We lived in three places—the school, the church and the skating rink—but our life was on the skating rink."[41]

That tradition endures. "This is the hub of our community," a resident of Manitou, Manitoba, population well under a thousand, told a reporter for the *Winnipeg Free Press*, referring to the skating rink. Many small towns in Canada construct and maintain hockey arenas at great cost to the community in both money and volunteer labor. The small town of Pierson, in the southwest corner of Manitoba, for example, supports its rink with an annual craft sale. The alternative is the demise of the community. "It's not the closing of a church or school or post office," according to Bernie Van De Walle, a Canadian historian. "When a town loses its rink, it loses its cultural center." In a country where, according to a 2015 survey, 90 percent of Canadians believe hockey is part of the nation's cultural fabric, the local rink is the heartbeat of the community. "The skating rink is every town's cathedral," Van De Walle says. "Every town that doesn't have a rink is either dead or dying." When the ice arena in the tiny town of Radisson, Saskatchewan, fell into disrepair in the 1980s, local citizens were frantic. "We know of other towns that have lost their rinks," one resident said. "The towns die overnight."[42]

As Leslie McFarlane observed in 1935, "hockey is more than a game; it is almost a religion." Eight decades later, the head of the Manitou Community Arena concurred. "That's where everyone gathers on Sunday," he said. "At the rinks."[43]

The Canadian claim on hockey was both imperiled and solidified in September 1972 during the Summit Series between a group of Soviet amateur players who faced off against a group of Canadian professionals, dubbed "the greatest hockey team ever assembled." When the Soviets arrived in Montréal for the first four games, Canadians were confident that, hockey being Canada's game, Team Canada would dispatch the Soviets handily. "The thing about hockey in Canada as opposed to hockey in other countries," Douglas Coupland wrote in *Souvenir of Canada*, "is that the sport percolates far deeper into our national soul and thus affects everything that grows in it."[44]

Team Canada's loss, 7–3, in the first game was a jolt to Canadian pride and sensibilities. One observer characterized the defeat as a "national castration," and the *Montréal Star* editorialized the following day: "Hockey is more than a game to Canadians, because it is—or so we fondly supposed until Saturday night—the one form of human endeavor in which we are the world's best. It is an important ingredient of our national pride, and an expression of our national character."[45]

The Summit Series headed for Moscow with the Soviets ahead 2–1, with one tie. Canada lost game five, falling further behind, but rallied in the following two games so that the teams entered the deciding eighth game tied, with each team posting a 3–3–1 record. For more than a few Canadians, from the Maritimes to the Pacific, nothing less than national identity was at stake. Only a last-minute goal by Paul Henderson, with thirty-four seconds remaining, secured a victory for Canada in the Summit Series; some Canadians still refer to it as "the goal of the century."

Foster Hewitt (1902–1985) was the voice of *Hockey Night in Canada*, providing a kind of "call to worship" on Saturday nights for Canadians from the Pacific to the Maritimes. Doug Griffin for *Toronto Star* via Getty Images.

Most Canadians of a certain age can tell you where they were when Henderson scored that goal, Bernie Van De Walle says, comparing it to the John F. Kennedy assassination or the *Challenger* disaster for Americans. As one historian observed, "The series did more for national unity than a dozen royal commissions and any number of constitutional conferences." Hockey once again was Canada's game.[46]

No phenomenon illustrates the communal dimension of Canada's game better than the *Hockey Night in Canada* broadcast; in religious terms, it is the sporting equivalent of a congregation assembling for worship. On Saturday nights, beginning on November 12, 1931, Canadians gathered around their radios to listen to the *General Motors Hockey Broadcast*, with Foster Hewitt providing play-by-play with his signature line, "He shoots, he scores!" The Canadian Broadcasting Corporation took over the radio program in 1936, rebranding it *Hockey Night in Canada*. The broadcast expanded to television on October 11, 1952, making it Canada's longest-running television program and the longest-running television sports program anywhere.[47]

Although ratings are down from those of previous decades, *Hockey Night in Canada* still unites Canadians across the nation. A congregation of the faithful, roughly a million strong, gathers every Saturday night—blue collar and white collar, Prairie Provinces and the Maritimes, First Nations and immigrants, Anglos and Francophones. As Stephen Marche writes, "In hockey, the Alberta construction worker and the Saskatchewan farmer and the Montréal lawyer and the Toronto businessman and businesswoman catch the flash of the *métis* dream of belonging to the North, of being *homme-du-nord*."[48]

Because hockey is a direct descendent of lacrosse, originally known as "baggataway," it would be reasonable to assume that Indigenous players would populate the rosters of organized hockey. Of the nearly eight thousand players in the history of the National Hockey League, however, fewer than a hundred claim a First Nations heritage.[49]

The Winnipeg Victorias team that won the Stanley Cup in 1901 and 1902 included three Métis players: Tony Gingras and the brothers Magnus and Rod Flett. A defenseman named Paul Jacobs, a Mohawk who excelled in both lacrosse and hockey, was on the Toronto Arenas roster for 1918–19. Another Mohawk, Henry Elmer "Buddy" Maracle, played eleven regular season and four playoff games for the New York Rangers in 1930–31, and Jim Jamieson, a Cayuga, played a single game for the Rangers in 1944. Fred Sasakamoose, a Cree who learned hockey at St. Michael's, a boarding school in Duck Lake, Saskatchewan, played center for the Chicago Black Hawks in 1953–54. On Saturday nights, Sasakamoose recalled in 2018, a priest at St. Michael's would rig up a speaker so that the students could listen to *Hockey Night in Canada*.[50]

Other notable Indigenous players in the NHL include Reginald "Reggie" Leach, an Ojibwe from Riverton, Manitoba; Bryan Trottier from Saskatchewan, whose father was Cree; and George Armstrong of northern Ontario, whose mother was Iroquois. Armstrong was captain of the Toronto Maple Leafs for a dozen years, a tenure that included four Stanley Cups.[51]

"I think we as First Nations people are probably some of the biggest supporters of hockey across Canada," Leach told the *New York Times* in 2018. This was not always the case, but anecdotal evidence suggests that Indigenous players are taking up the sport—one derived from their own game—in greater numbers.[52]

The story of hockey, including its earlier iteration as lacrosse, illustrates the transition from vernacular sport to regulated sport, which in turn can be seen as a tool of colonization and socialization. Just as W. George Beers, a Presbyterian, routinized the rules for lacrosse, so too in a larger sense sports helped to tame frontier passions. Schools and churches supported organized and regulated sports, which had the added benefit of reducing class tensions.

On the flip side, hockey also played a role in the less-than-benign assimilation of Indigenous peoples into Canadian culture. For more than a century, until 1998, the Canadian government snatched First Nations children away from their parents and forced them into residential schools, most of them run by religious organizations. Those institutions, similar to the Carlisle Indian Industrial School in Pennsylvania, undertook the mission of scrubbing Indigenous identity from their students, forcing them to cut their hair, wear European-style clothing, and speak only English and French. But these boarding schools also introduced First Nations children, like Sasakamoose, to hockey—thereby creating a cruel cultural paradox: The very same physical activity that First Nation peoples introduced to European immigrants, baggataway, evolved into a game that became a tool for the assimilation of Indigenous peoples into the dominant European-Canadian culture.[53]

Despite this tragic paradox, hockey, which emerged at the time of the Canadian Confederation, was nevertheless a democratic sport. Skates were relatively inexpensive, either to rent or buy, and anyone learning to skate quickly found that social pretensions did nothing to keep one upright on the ice. Skating, according to a handbook published by the Brooklyn Skating Rink Association for the 1868–69 season, "is particularly suited to our republican ideas."[54]

Hockey retains its rough edges, consistent with the wild Canadian landscape. "Hockey is the quintessential Canadian art form," according to Edward R. Grenda, "reflecting the indomitable elan and resolution in which Canadians, past and present, have tackled their severe winters." Roy MacGregor, a journalist, and Ken Dryden, a former player and politician, take a similar view. "Hockey is Canada's game," they write. "It is a place where the monumental themes of Canadian life are played out— English and French, East and West, Canada and the U.S., Canada and the world, the timeless tensions of commerce and culture, our struggle to survive and civilize winter."[55]

Even the game's "domestication" into arenas did not materially alter the fabric of hockey or its essential Canadian character. "The first organized game in Montréal legitimized hockey while covering it from the sky, removing it from the pond, narrowing its force, enclosing its spirit in rules," Stephen Marche writes. "Hockey became manageable, civilized, urbanized, brought within the walls, but that is Canada, too—a country of wild boys and girls who need to be civilized. The wildness at the heart of the game disturbs us and also refreshes us." The players' tradition of growing beards during the playoff run to the Stanley Cup, Marche believes, "mirrors the voyageurs' ritualistic journey up water, and, just like the voyageurs, hockey players become wilder and wilder as they progress through the playoffs."[56]

Hockey is an ancient game modernized, a blend of tradition and technology. The sticks were fashioned by First Nations people, and the skates became ever more technologically sophisticated; the number of patents for ice skates increased from 17 in the 1850s to 149 during the 1860s. It is the only major team sport not to use a ball. But for all of its evolution—from baggataway on open fields to armored players cruising up and down the ice—hockey retains a measure of the violence and lawlessness that characterizes the Canadian frontier. "Hockey is the Canadian metaphor," Bruce Kidd and John Macfarlane wrote in 1972, "the rink a symbol of this country's vast stretches of water and wilderness, its extremes of climate, the player a symbol of our struggle to civilize such a land." Indeed, the games may take place in an enclosed and regulated rink whose rounded edges recall countless windswept skating ponds, but the game as well as the venue plays on Canada's huge expanses of space. Canada's extremes of climate are replicated in the chilly hockey arena, and the ever-present specter of violence in hockey is reminiscent of the fact that, in a vast and uncharted frontier, players ultimately pursue their own vigilante justice; the vested authorities merely adjudicate matters after the fact.[57]

As W. George Beers noted, Canadian sports have a character of their own.

A Labyrinth of Wanderings

Urbanization and the Origins of Basketball

Whenever I witness games in a church league, I feel that my vision, almost half a century ago, of the time when the Christian people would recognize the true value of athletics, has become a reality.

—JAMES NAISMITH

When it's played the way it's supposed to be played, basketball happens in the air, flying, floating, elevated above the floor, levitating, the way oppressed peoples of this earth imagine themselves in their dreams.

—KAREEM ABDUL-JABBAR

For Canadians everywhere, and especially for residents of Ontario, Thursday night, June 11, 2019, was a time for celebration. Behind the magnificent play of Kawhi Leonard, the Toronto Raptors defeated the favored Golden State Warriors to win the National Basketball Association championship 4–2 in a best-of-seven series, marking the first time that a Canadian team claimed the NBA title. Although the league had established teams in two Canadian cities in 1996, the Vancouver Grizzlies decamped to Memphis following the 2000–2001 season, leaving only the Raptors north of the border.

The Raptors, who adopted the slogan "We the North," had contended for a championship several times before, advancing deep into the playoffs, but 2019 marked the first time they competed in the finals. Their victory ended the drought, and it also brought the Larry O'Brien Championship Trophy very close to the birthplace of basketball itself—in proximity, at least, to the little community that inspired the game.

Like hockey, the game of basketball has its roots in Canada. Unlike hockey, little controversy surrounds the origins of basketball.

Born in Ramsey, Ontario, in 1861, James Naismith was the second of three children. His father, a builder, moved the family to Almonte a few years later and still later to a small village, Grand Calumet Island, on the Ottawa River. In 1870, within the space of four months, Naismith lost his grandfather and both of his parents. Orphaned at age nine, James was reared by his grandmother and his uncle, a bachelor, in Bennies Corners, a community near Almonte in the northern reaches of Ontario.[1]

Naismith remembered watching his playmates skating on Indian River. He had no skates, but he retired to his uncle's shop and crafted a pair of skates from files set into hickory wood. In warmer weather, Naismith and other boys in town played a game they called duck-on-a-rock. A rock was placed atop a boulder, and the boys threw stones in an attempt knock the "duck" (rock) off the boulder. One boy was assigned the task of defending the duck.

In the fall of 1883, Naismith left Almonte to study for the ministry at McGill University in Montréal. By his own account, Naismith spent most of his time reading; he installed a small sign in his room: "Do not let anybody work harder today than I do." One evening, two upperclassmen visited his room and upbraided Naismith for neglecting physical activity; he responded by integrating regular visits to the gymnasium and the athletic field into his regimen.[2]

On the way back from a visit to downtown, Naismith stopped to watch the McGill football team practice. The center had broken his nose, and the captain invited Naismith to replace him. Naismith played his first game of college football the following Saturday against Queen's University. He never missed a game for seven years thereafter, even though many thought football a "tool of the devil" and not a proper pursuit for a student of theology. Naismith discovered, to his amusement, that a group of fellow divinity students had gathered to pray for his soul.[3]

Naismith secured his bachelor's degree in 1887 and promptly enrolled in Presbyterian College at McGill, all the while continuing his athletics. When the university's physical education director, Frederick Barnjum, died, Naismith took over the director's classes.

At some point during his time at McGill, Naismith wandered into the local YMCA. The Young Men's Christian Association had been formed by George Williams in London on June 6, 1844, to "win souls to Christ" and also to assist young men in their transition to urban life during the Industrial Revolution by developing a healthy "body, mind, and spirit"— illustrated by the "Y" triangle. The organization provided prayer groups and, later, accommodations and recreation as part of a program to keep young men out of trouble by keeping them off the streets. The YMCA expanded to Australia in 1850 and came to North America in 1851, first to Montréal, then to Boston, initially at Old South Church.

As Naismith was pondering his future, a conversation with the YMCA secretary in Montréal, D. A. Budge, persuaded him that "there might be other effective ways of doing good besides preaching." After completing his theological studies in 1890 and undertaking a tour of YMCAs in the United States and Canada, Naismith headed for Springfield, Massachusetts, to enroll in the International YMCA Training School (now Springfield College), persuaded that "the man who took his part in a manly way and yet kept his thoughts and conduct clean had the respect and the confidence of the most careless." Naismith added, "It was a short step to the conclusion that hard clean athletics could be used to set a high standard of living for the young."[4]

At Springfield, Naismith befriended a theological student from Yale, Amos Alonzo Stagg, also a student at the Training School. Before their first football game, Stagg offered a prayer that every player would do his best and demonstrate true Christian spirit. The undersized team, which competed against Yale, Harvard, Amherst, and other collegiate powerhouses, became known as "Stagg's Stubby Christians." As he had done at McGill, Naismith played center; Staggs placed him there, he told Naismith, "because you can do the meanest things in the most gentlemanly manner."[5]

Both Naismith and Staggs completed their studies in a year, and both were asked to stay on as instructors. In 1891, Luther Halsey Gulick, dean and head of the physical education department at the school, challenged Naismith to invent an indoor game that could be played in a small space, one that would be, in Naismith's words, "easy to play in the winter and by artificial light." Students were tired of gymnastics, and Gulick, son of Congregationalist missionaries to Hawai'i, was looking for a game that would occupy students during the winter months, between the football and the baseball seasons. "Doctor," Naismith replied, "we can invent a new game that will meet our needs. All that we have to do is to take the factors of our known games and recombine them, and we will have the game we are looking for."[6]

Gulick dispatched Naismith to Martha's Vineyard to observe and to consult with a Swedish physiologist, Nils Posse, but that foray produced little. Back in Springfield, the eighteen students in one particular class were becoming restive. They cycled through two instructors, impatient with gymnastics and marching in formation. "Here again, the men were given exercise in which they had no interest," Naismith observed in a faculty meeting during which the class, known as the "incorrigibles," was being discussed. "The trouble is not with the men, but with the system we are using." After a long silence, Gulick turned to Naismith and said, "Naismith, I want you to take that class and see what you can do with it." In the hallway afterward, Gulick told his protégé, "Now would be a good time for you to work on that new game you said could be invented."[7]

Over the ensuing fortnight, Naismith tried with no success to adapt lacrosse, rugby, and soccer to the indoor arena. Finally, at the edge of despair, Naismith reached back to his childhood game, duck-on-a-rock. He asked the superintendent of buildings at the school for two boxes, about eighteen inches square. "I'm figuring out a game," Naismith explained, "and I need the boxes to put on poles, so that a large ball can be thrown into them." Pop Stebbins, the superintendent, instead located two old peach baskets, which Naismith affixed on the lower rail of the gymnasium balcony, ten feet above the floor. The ball at hand was a soccer ball. He returned to his office and in the space of an hour drafted thirteen rules for the new game.[8]

From the inception of the game, Naismith, perhaps recalling the brutality of football, sought to stem violence on the court. The goal would be vertical, not horizontal, he decided, and players could not run with

James Naismith (1861–1939) invented basketball at the YMCA School for Christian Workers (now Springfield College) in response to a challenge to devise a game that would occupy young men between the football and baseball seasons. Picturenow via Getty Images.

the ball. "If he can't run with the ball, we don't have to tackle," Naismith wrote, "and if we don't have to tackle, the roughness will be eliminated." Rule number five in his Thirteen Rules of the game read in part: "No shouldering, holding, pushing, or tripping, or striking, in any way the person of an opponent shall be allowed; the first infringement of this rule by any person shall count as a foul."[9]

The date was December 21, 1891, and Naismith anxiously briefed the "incorrigibles" on the new, as yet unnamed, game. "I was sure in my mind that the game was good, but it needed a real test," Naismith recalled. "I felt that its success or failure depended largely on the way the class received it."[10]

The first game of basketball was played with nine players to a side, in the sixty-by-thirty-five-foot gymnasium (considerably less than half the size of today's regulation basketball court). It was a success. "The players seemed to heartily enjoy the rough and tumble of the game," Naismith recorded, "especially the effort to keep from personal contact with the opponents." Stebbins, the building superintendent, was on hand with a ladder to retrieve the ball from the basket, but the ball made it into a basket only once, a twenty-five-foot shot from William Chase, who would go on to become a YMCA secretary. The "incorrigibles" enjoyed the game so much that they wanted to keep playing even when the class period was over.[11]

As word of the new game spread across campus, spectators began to assemble. A group of women asked if they could play; Naismith saw no reason why they shouldn't. He arranged times when the women could use the gym. Players were drawn from the ranks of secretaries and faculty wives; one of the stenographers was Maude Simpson, Naismith recalled, "whom I later asked to become Mrs. Naismith."[12]

Later, Senda Berenson, director of physical education at Smith College, became interested in the new game and visited Naismith in nearby Springfield to learn more about it. On March 21, 1893, Berenson organized the first women's collegiate basketball game, which the *Springfield Republican* reported as a match between the freshman and sophomore teams at Smith. (Male spectators were not allowed because the women wore bloomers.) Another women's school, Bryn Mawr College, took up the game, and the *San Francisco Examiner* reported in 1895 on a women's game between Stanford and the University of California, Berkeley. The newspaper called it "a Homeric Contest," and the article's subtitle read, "Clad in Bloomers and Sweaters, Muscular Maidens Struggle for Supremacy."[13]

Naismith approved. Looking back on his invention several decades later, he wrote, "In my estimation, girls have made far greater strides in physical education in the past twenty-five years than boys."[14]

Following the Christmas break after Naismith had introduced basketball to the "incorrigibles," a colleague asked if he had a name for the new game. When Naismith said no, the colleague suggested Naismith Ball.

Smith College Class of 1895 basketball team. In 1893, Smith students were among the first to play basketball. Miriam and Ira D. Wallach Division of Art, Prints and Photographs, Photography Collection, New York Public Library.

Naismith demurred. "We have a basket and a ball," the colleague replied. "How about basket ball?" The name persisted as two words until 1921, when sportswriters conflated it to "basketball."[15]

The very first game prefigured basketball's international appeal. The "incorrigibles" class included a student from France, another from Japan, and a third from Britain, three Americans, and four Canadians. By October 1892, less than a year after the game's invention, Luther Gulick wrote, "It is doubtful whether a gymnastic game has ever spread so rapidly over the continent as 'basket ball.' It is played from New York to San Francisco." T. D. Patton, one of the "incorrigibles," who hailed from Toronto, introduced basketball to India in 1894.[16]

Once basketball caught on at the Training School, the students became its most fervent ambassadors; members of the "incorrigibles" class demonstrated the new game at local YMCAs during school breaks. Fanning out as directors of YMCAs across North America and eventually the world, graduates of the Springfield school introduced basketball far and wide. In addition, athletic clubs, settlement houses, Indian schools, military institutions, mission fields, and churches took up the game. Naismith, himself a fervent disciple of Muscular Christianity, couldn't have been more pleased. Basketball was a game that also bridged religious boundaries. The Knights of Columbus and the Catholic Youth Organization picked it up, as did the Young Men's Hebrew Association. Still later, basketball would be played by Muslims, including converts to Islam: Hakeem Olajuwon, Mahmoud Abdul-Rauf, Al-Farouq Aminu, and most famously, Kareem Abdul-Jabbar, who grew up Lew Alcindor in upper Manhattan.[17]

Naismith himself was gratified at the success and the geographical reach of his game. "I am sure that no man can derive more satisfaction from money or power than I do from seeing a pair of basketball goals in some out of the way place," he recalled. "Deep in the Wisconsin woods, an old barrel hoop nailed to a tree. High in the Colorado mountains, a pair of crude backstops; halfway across the desert, a crude iron ring fastened to a weather-beaten barn—all are constant reminders that I have at least partially accomplished the objective that I set up."[18]

Naismith may have appreciated the reach of basketball into rural communities, and it is true that the game is played extensively by Native Americans on Indian reservations. But the real home for basketball is the city. Alone among the four major team sports, it is played on hardwood (or asphalt, on playgrounds) rather than on a field; it has in that way adapted to, even capitalized on, its urban environment. More important, basketball is the quintessential urban game whose object it is for players to maneuver in a constricted space without impeding the movements of others.[19]

Naismith, who believed the game could teach moral lessons, invented basketball at a time when Americans were flocking to the cities. Between 1860 and 1920, the urban population in the United States overall swelled from 6.2 million to 54.3 million. Within the space of twenty years, 1880 to 1900, cities grew by about 15 million people; New York City expanded from 1.9 million inhabitants to 3.4 million, Chicago increased from 503,000 to 1.7 million, and Boston nearly doubled in size. In 1870, only two American cities had a population of more than five hundred thousand; by 1900, there were six, and three of these—New York, Chicago, and Philadelphia—had more than a million inhabitants each.[20]

American Protestants in the final decade of the nineteenth century clearly perceived the growth of the cities as a source of danger. The influx of non-Protestant immigrants, most of whom did not share Protestant scruples about temperance, made for a perilous, anxious, chaotic place. No one captured this sense of danger better than Jacob Riis, a Danish-born journalist in New York City. His photojournalistic forays into the tenements on the Lower East Side of Manhattan were certainly voyeuristic and riddled with ethnic essentialism, but they also laid bare the squalor of those who resided in cramped, infested quarters. The number of saloons below Fourteenth Street, Riis famously calculated, was exponentially larger than the number of churches.

Protestant theology, especially Reformed theology (Calvinism), understood this anxiety. "God succors us when he sees us oppressed by anxious thoughts," John Calvin wrote. Anxiety, Calvin believed, stemmed in part from the absence of boundaries: "The whole life of man is a ruinous labyrinth of wanderings." In a chaotic context such as a city, it was essential to designate boundaries, and within those limitations, individuals could more readily navigate the jumble of urban space.[21]

Calvin, then, understood the world as a labyrinth, and the believer's task was to negotiate his way through the complexities of that world, a metaphor echoed by John Bunyan in *The Pilgrim's Progress* and embodied by life in the city. Naismith was a Presbyterian, the denomination more than any other associated with Reformed, or Calvinist, theology. He was almost surely aware of these metaphors, and the skills that Naismith believed would be enhanced by the game of basketball might double as spiritual attributes: initiative, cooperation, self-control, accuracy, and self-sacrifice.

Naismith's game provided boundaries—ninety-four by fifty feet, to be precise—and the task of the players was to negotiate the labyrinth of other players within that constricted space, not unlike a pedestrian wending her way along a crowded boulevard. "Both of the contesting teams occupy the same space on the floor," Naismith wrote in describing the fundamental principles of the game, "and often the teams are so intermingled that it is hard to distinguish one from another."[22]

Naismith also understood his game, at least implicitly, as an evolutionary advance over other sports. "Basketball was intended primarily for young men who had acquired their physical development," he wrote, "but who were in need of exercise that would stress the skills and agile movements that were lacking in manual labor." Basketball together with sportsmanship, for Naismith, offered a refinement of physical skills—agility over brute force—and as such it prepared players for success in the newly emerging urban environment.

Just prior to his statement about "skills and agile movements," Naismith recounted his experience with Johnny Williams, a talented player at the Denver YMCA, where Naismith worked while studying medicine at Gross Medical School. Williams, despite his manifest abilities, was a hothead. "He would play brilliant ball," Naismith recalled, "but eventually he would lose his temper and be told to leave the floor, many times when he was most needed." Naismith called Williams into his office and admonished him to curb his temper in the interests of the team. "By the end of the season he had so successfully learned to control his feelings that he was the mainstay of the team," Naismith reported. "His mates unanimously elected him captain for the following year."[23]

Naismith went on to list the attributes that basketball develops; most of them—initiative, accuracy, alertness, cooperation, self-confidence, self-sacrifice, self-control—might also fill the pages of a self-help book for an up-and-coming urban worker at the turn of the twentieth century, qualities that manual labor alone could not have cultivated. Years after Naismith's initial encounter with Williams, the hotheaded basketball player, the two met again in Denver during a session of the Colorado legislature. Williams had been elected as a representative, and he thanked Naismith for having "helped him overcome a fault that would have been a serious drawback throughout his life."[24]

Basketball's connection to Springfield, Chicago, and New York, as well as its general and persistent popularity in cities, suggests the symbolic meaning behind the game. Basketball is the quintessential urban game, where the object is to maneuver in tight quarters without impeding the movements of others. Any such obstruction, as Naismith stipulated in his Thirteen Rules, would be called a foul. Naismith had specified this among the five fundamental principles he considered in devising the game. "Both teams are to occupy the same area," he wrote, "yet there is to be no personal contact."[25]

This challenge was especially daunting in the early years of the game. Because of the size of Naismith's physical education class, the first basketball games pitted nine players on one team against a similar number on the other, eighteen players total, and some contemporary accounts tell of games with fifty players on a team, all maneuvering within the constricted space of a gymnasium that was less than half the size of a regulation basketball court.[26]

There are, to be sure, ethereal elements to the game. A shot at the basket arcs high into the air, and the players themselves sometimes appear to defy gravity, their levitations providing a brief escape from gravitational pull and the horizontal plane of city streets. But basketball is grounded in the urban experience, and it emerged just at the moment that Americans were moving to the cities in large numbers, where they encountered a bewildering mass of humanity tucked into a limited space. Anyone who has sought to navigate Times Square in the evening, Michigan Avenue at rush hour, or Fifth Avenue at noontime understands the parallel between basketball and urban life. The challenge of threading one's way through a small, defined space toward a distant goal requires a spontaneous combination of athleticism, artistry, evasiveness, and guile. These are the qualities that define a good basketball player.

The twin factors of urbanization and industrialization, especially when coupled with immigration, fundamentally recast American cities at about the same time that Naismith invented basketball. A second migratory wave after the turn of the twentieth century, the movement of African Americans from the South to northern cities, known as the Great

Migration, was equally transformative—and, once again, basketball played a role.[27]

The catalysts for the Great Migration were many. Black codes and Jim Crow laws persisted in the South. African Americans faced poverty, discrimination in education and employment, and no assurance of justice in white-dominated courtrooms. A round of crop failures coupled with a resurgence of racism, especially the second iteration of the Ku Klux Klan in the 1910s and 1920s, provided further reasons to look to the North. Word had filtered south that jobs were available in the expanding cities, some to replace soldiers who were fighting World War I, others as labor scabs.

Migration tended to follow the train lines in a north-south axis. African Americans from Georgia and the Carolinas, for example, headed north to Newark and New York City, while Black people from Alabama and the Mississippi Delta traveled through Memphis on their way to Chicago or Detroit. The new world that greeted them was not always kind. Returning soldiers reclaimed their jobs, and the onset of the Great Depression left nearly everyone out of work.

Once again, the YMCA assisted young men in their transition to urban life. Naismith's invention of basketball in 1891 was part of the recreational focus of the movement, although the emphasis had been on gymnastics prior to the emergence of the new game. Basketball teams and leagues cropped up in YMCAs across North America. Swimming lessons were first introduced at the Toronto YMCA in 1906 and three years later in Detroit.

In 1853, the first YMCA for African Americans, later known as the Twelfth Street YMCA, was founded in Washington, D.C., by Anthony Bowen, a freed slave and minister in the African Methodist Episcopal Church. The National Council of the YMCA established a Colored Work Department in 1890, and in 1910, Julius Rosenwald, head of Sears, Roebuck and Company, announced a challenge grant to construct YMCAs in Black communities. Twenty-five African American YMCAs were established in twenty-three cities, and as Black people funneled into northern cities during the Great Migration, the YMCA was there to help in the transition to urban life. In Chicago by the mid-1920s, for example, the fifty-one YMCAs in the city counted twenty-eight thousand African

Founded in Britain as a way to help young men acclimate to urban life, the YMCA played a similar role for African Americans during the Great Migration early in the twentieth century. This photograph shows an all-Black YMCA team during the 1909–10 season. Schomburg Center for Research in Black Culture, Jean Blackwell Hutson Research and Reference Division, New York Public Library.

American members. The "Y" provided housing and job training, and it was often a center for African American life. Carter G. Woodson, an African American historian, organized the Association for the Study of Negro Life and History at the Wabash YMCA in Chicago in 1915, the precursor to Negro History Week and, eventually, Black History Month. Langston Hughes lived at the Twelfth Street YMCA in Washington, and Thurgood Marshall plotted his arguments for *Brown v. Board of Education* there. In 1920, Andrew "Rube" Foster and a group of African American team owners formed the Negro National League at the Paseo YMCA in Kansas City.[28]

YMCAs also provided recreation for African Americans, including an introduction to basketball. From 1904 until 1950, when the National Basketball Association was finally integrated, all-Black basketball teams and leagues were organized out of African American YMCAs. The teams were customarily called "Black Fives" or "Negro Fives" or "Colored Fives," sometimes as "Colored Quints." The game soon expanded beyond the

YMCAs, notably with the formation of the Alpha Physical Culture Club of Harlem in 1904 by three Jamaican-born brothers. "We were helping our race by fortifying the bodies of our people in this, the struggle for existence," one of the brothers said, "where only the fittest survive." In 1907, three African American teams (one of them a church team) formed the Olympian Athletic League, eventually joined by a fourth team, the Alpha Big Five, from the Alpha Physical Culture Club. By 1910 the Alpha Big Five was playing before crowds in excess of a thousand at the Manhattan Casino in Harlem, where the games were punctuated at halftime and after the game by other entertainment, principally singing and dancing. The Alpha Club added a women's basketball team, the New York Girls.[29]

By the 1920s Black Fives were playing in competitive leagues in New York, Washington, Philadelphia, and Chicago. But the popularity of the game wasn't limited to YMCAs and competitive leagues. The urban game of basketball was perfectly suited to confined spaces such as playgrounds or indoor gymnasiums, and Naismith had specified that he wanted a game that would not be expensive for the participants. The peach baskets in Springfield eventually gave way to hoops mounted on poles, but as long as a ball was at hand, the game could be played.

And it was. Basketball took root in the urban environment at the turn of the twentieth century—in YMCA and church gymnasiums, but also in schoolyards, on playgrounds, and even in the streets. Each neighborhood, from Rockaway to Cabrini Green, from Harlem to Bedford-Stuyvesant, from Roxbury to Mattapan, had its playgrounds as well as its own pecking orders and protocols to determine who played when and against whom. And each neighborhood also reverberated with tales of its own legends, players of extraordinary grace and talent who, for one reason or another, sometimes tragic—injury or drugs or inadequate grades or family responsibilities—never quite made the transition to the klieg lights of college arenas or Madison Square Garden. In the telling and retelling of their feats among the neighborhood cognoscenti, the names of those players—Willie Parker, Clinton Robinson, Herman "Helicopter" Knowings, Pablo Robertson, Earl Manigault, Kenny Bellinger, and countless others—assumed mythic status.[30]

"Basketball is the city game," sportswriter Pete Axthelm observed. "Its battlegrounds are strips of asphalt between tattered wire fences or crumbling buildings; its rhythms grow from the uneven thump of a ball against hard surfaces." The absence of elaborate equipment effectively democratized the sport. "Basketball is the game for young athletes without cars or allowances," Axthelm wrote, "the game whose drama and action are intensified by its confined spaces and chaotic surroundings."[31]

As Onaje X. O. Woodbine discovered upon returning to Boston after his basketball sojourn at Yale, the urban basketball court is ritual space, where young men, including African American men, could retreat from the turmoil of ghetto life, the violence of the streets, and dysfunctional (or nonexistent) families. "I remember just being on that floor and it was just basketball," one player told Woodbine about a game following a family tragedy. "I was just numb to the surroundings. I was playing, it was a beautiful thing. I was just playing." Basketball provides identity. "It has been the tool to my life to make me who I am," another player declared. "Without it, I don't know if I would be who I am." Clergy from local Black churches use basketball tournaments to broker peace among competing gangs, and basketball also provides a vehicle for grieving friends and fellow players whose lives have been lost to violence.[32]

In an era when small towns supported baseball and basketball teams, a young, aspiring impresario saw an opportunity. Born in London, Abraham M. Saperstein attended Chicago's public schools and in 1926 secured a job in the city's Wells Park recreation center, a job that included coaching basketball. He briefly served as booking agent for an African American basketball team called Tommy Brookins's Globe Trotters, and in 1927, the diminutive Saperstein took over an all-Black team called the Savoy Big Five, named after Chicago's Savoy Ballroom. Although neither Saperstein nor his players had any connection to New York City, they adopted the name "Harlem, New York, Globe Trotters" and barnstormed throughout the Midwest and eventually the nation and the world.[33]

Because the Globetrotters were so good, Abe Saperstein increasingly had difficulty finding opponents, so he added trick plays and razzle-dazzle antics to the show. Still, the Globetrotters were a talented team, and their athletic success led to social change. On February 19, 1948, not fully a year after Jackie Robinson broke the color barrier in Major League Baseball, the Globetrotters beat George Mikan and the powerhouse Minneapolis

At Chicago Stadium on February 19, 1948, the Harlem Globetrotters defeated the
Minneapolis Lakers and their star, George Mikan (1924–2005), second from left, in an
exhibition game that drew the highest attendance of any sporting event in the city's
history to that point. This showcase of African American talent contributed to the drafting
of Black players into the NBA two years later. Other players in this photo from a 1950
rematch are, from left, Nat "Sweetwater" Clifton (1922–1990), Louis "Babe" Pressley,
(1916–1965) and Slater "Dugie" Martin (1925–2012). Charles Knoblock, AP Images.

Lakers with a last-second shot in an exhibition game at Chicago Stadium.
The game had the highest attendance of any professional game in the city
to that point. Two years later, the National Basketball Association drafted
three African American players, and in 1958, Elgin Baylor, who learned
basketball at the Twelfth Street YMCA in Washington, D.C., was the first
overall draft pick for the NBA.[34]

"The records show that the Negro is an integral part of the development of the great sport of basketball," Charles H. Baltimore wrote in
1951, "and his proficiency, interest and participation in the game will

increase as more and more opportunities are opened for him to take part in the sport."[35]

One city kid who became enamored of the game was John McLendon, who graduated from Sumner High School in Kansas City. He decided as early as sixth grade that he wanted someday to be a basketball coach, and he set his eyes on the school in Springfield, Massachusetts, that had been the birthplace of basketball. After McLendon's father said that Springfield was too far away, he informed his son that the inventor of basketball itself taught just down the road at the University of Kansas, in Lawrence.

When the elder McLendon dropped his son off in Lawrence in the fall of 1933, he instructed him to find Naismith and introduce himself. "Tell him that he's to be your adviser," the father said. After a knock on the door and a brief introduction, Naismith asked John McLendon who had sent him. "My father," the first-year student said. "Fathers are always right," Naismith replied.[36]

Thus began a mentoring relationship that would endure for the remainder of Naismith's life. McLendon, who was half Native American and half African American, sometimes had trouble navigating the vaga-ries of an overwhelmingly white campus. Naismith assisted him when-ever possible. "Many of my doubts about being at Kansas were quickly dispelled by Dr. Naismith, who treated me courteously and attentively," McLendon recalled many years later, "and made me feel comfortable in my surroundings as a new student."[37]

Forrest "Phog" Allen's basketball teams at the University of Kansas were all white; McLendon tried out several times, but he was always cut. Instead, he absorbed from Naismith as much wisdom about the game as he could. "I used to go over to his house at night to talk about basketball and life," McLendon said. One day as the two of them were walking, they happened upon a pickup game where the players were running aggres-sively. Naismith opined that the game should be played like that all the time, both on offense and defense. "I patterned my whole game after that philosophy," McLendon recalled. He eventually translated that advice into a fast-break offense and a full-court defense, which would become the signature characteristics of his coaching career. "He taught me every-thing I know about basketball and physical education," McLendon said of

Naismith. "Everything I ever did when I was coaching, I can trace back to learning from him."[38]

As McLendon approached graduation at the University of Kansas, Naismith helped him secure a job coaching the Black basketball team at Lawrence High School, which went on to win the Kansas-Missouri Athletic Conference championship. From there, McLendon studied at the University of Iowa and landed a job as an assistant coach at North Carolina College for Negroes, in Durham; he was promoted to head coach in 1940, a year after Naismith's death.

McLendon's aggressive baseline-to-baseline strategy paid off. The North Carolina College Eagles won the Negro National College Championship in 1941, McLendon's first year as coach.

Three years later, after his team posted a 19–1 record, McLendon quietly approached the all-white intramural team at the neighboring Duke Medical School, a team comprised of graduate students, many of whom had competed in college. They agreed on an exhibition game, which was illegal under Jim Crow laws at the time. On a Sunday morning, March 19, 1944—Sunday because most of the locals would be in church—a carload of Duke medical students pulled onto the North Carolina College campus and found the gymnasium. With coats pulled over their heads to hide their identity, the players entered the building and changed into their uniforms. The doors of the gymnasium were locked behind them; even the school's president did not know about the game.[39]

The Eagles were nervous early on. Perhaps it was the novelty of the empty gymnasium, or the Duke players' fancy plays, or the lingering fear that the police or the Ku Klux Klan might catch wind of the game. There could be a knock on the door at any moment, and arrests would follow— or worse. The Duke team led by eight at halftime. After the half, however, the Eagles hit their stride with McLendon's signature full-court presses and fast breaks. The final score was a blowout: North Carolina College 88, Duke Medical School 44. "They shellacked us," one of the Duke players said about the first integrated college basketball game in the South.[40]

McLendon, with his up-tempo game, went on to a distinguished coaching career. He became the first Black coach of a professional basketball team, the Cleveland Pipers, and the first African American coach at a majority white college, Cleveland State University.[41]

A protégé of James Naismith, John McLendon (1915–1999) was not allowed to play on Phog Allen's all-white basketball team at the University of Kansas. But McLendon took Naismith's advice that basketball should be played up-tempo and translated that into a distinguished coaching career. In 1962, he became the first African American coach of a professional basketball team, the Cleveland Pipers. Bettmann via Getty Images.

Behind an all-Black starting five, the Texas Western Miners, coached by Don Haskins (1930–2008), second from left, defeated the all-white University of Kentucky 72–65 for the 1966 NCAA Basketball Championship. AP Images.

Another racial milestone took place on March 7, 1966, at the Cole Field House on the campus of the University of Maryland. For the first time in NCAA history, five Black players, starters for the Texas Western Miners, took the court for a championship game. Their opponents were the University of Kentucky Wildcats, coached by Adolph Rupp, who had already won four championships. The Kentucky team and coaches all were white, as were the referees, cheerleaders, and most of the fans. Kentucky boosters waved a Confederate flag from the stands. One writer called it "the *Brown v. Board of Education* game," in part because Rupp was an unreconstructed segregationist. Another sportswriter in the Kentucky locker room at halftime, when the Wildcats were trailing 34–31, quoted Rupp exhorting his players, "You've got to beat those coons." The Miners, however, coached by Don Haskins, a white former high school coach who had taken a pay cut to coach at Texas Western, prevailed 72–65 to win the NCAA championship. The following year, schools in the South began recruiting African American players—not only to expand their

talent pool but also to avoid the embarrassment that Rupp and his Wildcats suffered at the hands of Texas Western in College Park, Maryland.[42]

Although basketball had been played as an exhibition in the Olympics
as early as the St. Louis Olympics of 1904, it was not added as an official
competition until 1936, when the games were played in Berlin. Friends
of Naismith decided that basketball's founder should be present for the
occasion. At the behest of Phog Allen, coach of the Kansas basketball
team, the National Association of Basketball Coaches recommended that
during "Naismith Week" in February 1936, a penny from every ticket
sold at high school and collegiate basketball games should be set aside to
finance Naismith's travel to Berlin.[43]

Naismith, approaching his seventy-fifth birthday, had enjoyed a colorful, if somewhat unconventional, career. Although he earned a diploma
from the Presbyterian College at McGill, he was not ordained until 1916,
age fifty-four. Following Naismith's invention of basketball in Springfield, Massachusetts, he moved to Denver and earned a medical degree,
although he never practiced professionally as a physician. When the
University of Kansas contacted Amos Alonzo Stagg, football coach at
the University of Chicago, looking for a recommendation for someone
to lead the university chapel and also serve as head of the physical education department, Stagg quickly responded that Naismith was the ideal
candidate for the job. Naismith, he said, was the "inventor of basket-ball,
medical doctor, Presbyterian minister, tee-totaler, all-around athlete, non-
smoker, and owner of vocabulary without cuss words."[44]

Naismith accepted, filling the dual roles of chaplain and director
of athletics at the University of Kansas, thereby personifying the twin
emphases of Muscular Christianity: religion and sports. Naismith introduced basketball to the school and effectively became the team's coach,
although he was often more interested in other sports like fencing or
lacrosse. The inventor of basketball still holds the dubious distinction of
being the only basketball coach in the university's history with a losing
career record.

Although he declared himself "more pleased and excited than a farm
boy at his first circus," Naismith's foray across the Atlantic came at a
fraught historical moment. Since the Olympic committee had awarded

the games to Berlin in 1931, Adolf Hitler had come to power in Germany, and he sought to use the games as a showcase for Aryan supremacy. Jesse Owens, the American track star, frustrated those plans with four gold medals, but Naismith must certainly have felt uneasy about the situation. The inventor of basketball understood his as an inclusive game, racially and internationally. "Dr. Naismith didn't know anything about color or nationality," John McLendon, Naismith's Black protégé from the University of Kansas, recalled in 1979.[45]

Naismith managed to steer clear of controversy in Berlin. At the beginning of the basketball competition on August 7, the teams representing twenty-one countries filed past Naismith, the guest of honor, as his eyes welled with tears. He would later remember it as the single greatest moment of his life. "These boys were not all the same size nor the same color," his daughter recalled. "They didn't even speak the same language, but they all had one thing in common—basketball, his game." Naismith could also take satisfaction that the coaching staffs of the various competing teams included seventeen graduates of the YMCA Training School, in Springfield, Massachusetts, where basketball was born.[46]

The gold medal game pitted his native Canada against the United States, where Naismith had spent the majority of his life and had become a naturalized citizen. The United States prevailed 19–8. Basketball's founder presented the gold medals.

James Naismith, his legacy assured, died three years later. "I am not worried about the future of basketball," he once said, "because the game itself is interesting no matter how you fool with it. If a game is interesting, it will last, and basketball is just that."[47]

Shut Up and Dribble

From the Sanctuary to the Stadium

Being a sports fan is a complex matter, in part irrational but
not unworthy; a relief from the seriousness of the real world,
with its unending pressures and often grave obligations.

—RICHARD GILMAN

If there is a truly religious quality to sport, then, it lies first in the
intensity of devotion brought by the true believer, or fan. And
it consists, second, and much more so, in the widely shared,
binding nature—the creed-like quality of American sport.

—A. BARTLETT GIAMATTI

EastLake Community Church, an evangelical congregation in the Seattle suburb of Bothell, Washington, faced a dilemma. When the Seattle
Seahawks played away games in the Eastern time zone, the game was
broadcast at ten o'clock in the morning local (Pacific) time, the same
time as Sunday services. For Ryan Meeks, founding pastor of the church,
the solution was obvious. EastLake cancelled its ten o'clock service and
invited its fans/congregants to attend a specially scheduled service after
the game, at six o'clock Sunday evening.[1]

The story of EastLake and the Seahawks is not unique. Other churches
have made similar accommodations to sporting events. Whereas, in the
nineteenth and into the early twentieth centuries, Protestants railed

against Sunday sporting events as a violation of Sabbatarian scruples, now they struggle to compete, with Super Bowl–viewing parties and other programmatic concessions. "This is church," Stephen Jay Gould, no fan of organized religion, said about baseball, "and nonbelievers cannot know the spirit." The same applies north of the border. "While the religion of Canada is assuredly Christianity," Miriam Chapin wrote in 1959, "every fall when the football season opens, and every spring when the hockey play-offs come round, it begins to appear that the religion of Canadians is sport." William Kilbourn opened his *Religion in Canada* volume by observing, "If I were asked by some stranger to North American culture to show him the most important religious building in Canada, I would take him to Toronto's Maple Leaf Gardens."[2]

These sentiments illustrate shifting priorities in North America. The United States has long been one of the most religious nations in the world, with 89 percent of the population affirming their belief in God, according to the Pew Research Center in 2014. Canadians lag a bit, but they are not far behind: 76 percent claimed a religious affiliation in a 2011 survey. As impressive as those numbers are, especially as compared with France, Japan, or Great Britain, the percentage of the population that would be considered devout has fallen in recent years. One survey found that Americans who didn't associated with any religion (sometimes called "nones") grew from 5 percent to 23 percent between 1972 and 2018 and up to 28 percent in 2020. According to another survey, those considered religiously unaffiliated in the United States increased from 31 to 35 percent from 2007 to 2014; the number of unaffiliated younger Americans ages eighteen to twenty-nine grew to 38 percent in 2016. In Canada, the percentage of religiously unaffiliated increased from 4 to 24 percent over the course of four decades, between 1971 and 2011.[3]

If religious adherence has fallen somewhat in recent years, devotion to sports has not. Gallup found in 2015 that 59 percent of adults in the United States (66 percent of men and 51 percent of women) described themselves as sports fans. Viewing habits have changed in recent years—attendance, television, radio, mobile devices, virtual sports, fantasy leagues—but a passion for sports endures. Entire cable channels are devoted to sports, and sports radio provides another index of devotion. The medium has several progenitors, but the beginning of the

Mike Francesa (b. 1954), shown here in the early 1990s, was one of the pioneers of sports radio. Fans calling in to sports radio have an experience not unlike entering a confessional, including the ritual incantation "First time, longtime," short for first-time caller but longtime listener. New York Daily News Archive via Getty Images.

phenomenon is generally traced to June 30, 1987, when WFAN began broadcasting out of a basement studio in Queens, New York. By 2010 the station was taking in over $40 million in revenue, rising to $178.1 million in 2020. The number of sports-radio stations across the country increased to 500 by 2005 and to 677 in 2011. By 2013, according to the *Hollywood Reporter*, more than 27 million listeners were tuning in to sports radio every week, and in 2017 WFAN alone drew an average of 1.9 million listeners on any given day.[4]

In such a wildly, gorgeously multicultural society such as that in North America (both the United States and Canada), perhaps it's not surprising that sports has emerged as a meeting ground. As a friend once told me, "If I'm pumping gas, and a pickup truck pulls alongside with a New England Patriots bumper sticker, we have something to talk about—even though we might otherwise be at opposite ends of the political or socioeconomic spectrum and have nothing else in common." The vernacular of sports provides a common vocabulary, especially at a time when the centrifugal forces of race, ethnicity, religion, economics, media, and politics are tearing us apart. "Because no single formal religion can embrace a people who hold so many faiths, including no particular formal faith at all," A. Bartlett Giamatti observed in 1984, "sports and politics are the civil surrogates for a people ever in quest for a covenant."[5]

Whether politics still fills that role in the early decades of the twenty-first century is a matter of dispute. What is less debatable is that team sports emerged in the nineteenth century coincident with profound social changes—industrialism (baseball), war (football), nationalism (hockey), and urbanization (basketball)—and the development of those sports both reflected the zeitgeist and provided, in Giamatti's words, a civil surrogate to understand and to address those issues. In the decades straddling the turn of the twenty-first century, the issues are analogous, though perhaps not identical. Whereas the nineteenth century brought industrialization, workers now face economic dislocation wrought by globalization and the digital economy; nationalism has increased dramatically; urbanization has given way to worries about immigration; and war, sadly, is a constant. Once again, now as in an earlier era, the escapism offered by sports fandom provides a way to deal with—or to ignore—those issues.

Passion, whether directed toward sports or toward religion, doesn't submit easily to the metrics of quantification, let alone comparison. But it is at the very least not unreasonable to argue that sports in North America has become something that resembles religion, a phenomenon that generates at least as much devotion as traditional religions. Indeed, the two—sports and religion—share characteristics in common. Both are premised on an agreement on principles, although there may be disagreement over interpretation. For religion the basic principles might be, for example, the Four Noble Truths of Buddhism, the Five Pillars of Islam, or the Nicene Creed in Christianity; in sports, it is a set of rules. Similarly, the sacred text could be the official rulebook for hockey, baseball, basketball, or football; for religion, the Qur'an, the Hebrew Bible, the New Testament, or the sayings (*Analects*) of Confucius.

Both sports and religion have sacred spaces: Jerusalem, the holy city of Mecca, various shrines and temples, or St. Peter's Basilica for religion; sports fans might designate the stadium of their favorite teams, especially older and more venerable venues like Wrigley Field, Fenway Park, Lambeau Field in Green Bay, Wisconsin, the Forum in Montréal, or the "Big House" in Ann Arbor, Michigan. Followers of both sports and religion make pilgrimages to their sacred sites. As Scott Young observed in *The Boys of Saturday Night*, "Fans coming to Toronto for the first time trooped like pilgrims to Maple Leaf Gardens."[6]

Consider the March 15, 1996, procession down Sainte Catherine Street, the principal shopping district in Montréal. Four days earlier, prior to the final hockey game played at the Forum, home to the Montréal Canadiens since 1926, twenty-three former players gathered on the ice, including the legendary Maurice "The Rocket" Richard. The oldest surviving team captain, Émile "Butch" Bouchard, carrying a flaming torch, skated to center ice. He then passed the torch hand to hand to other Canadiens captains, thereby claiming the winning tradition—twenty-four Stanley Cups—that had been associated with both the building and the team. Then, four days later, that torch, together with ice scrapings from the Forum, was part of a two-mile procession, complete with a giant inflated Canadiens player, from the Forum to the new arena, Molson Centre. New Stanley Cup banners were hung, the Forum ice (now water) was sprinkled over the Molson Centre ice in a rite reminiscent of baptism, and the current team captain dipped the torch to the team's logo on center ice. Some elements of this ritual tableau, which took place in the context of French Catholic Québec, may have been ham-handed, bordering on hokey, but for anyone familiar with Roman Catholic rituals—the transfer of saints' relics, the deconsecration and consecration of sacred space, and the street processions where a statue of the Blessed Virgin was paraded through ethnic neighborhoods—the meaning and the purpose was clear: the transfer of sacrality—and tradition and luck and karma—from one venue to another.[7]

Ritual is associated with both religion and sports. The choreographed entry of football teams from the stadium tunnel onto the field, often accompanied by smoke, is not very different from a liturgical procession,

On March 15, 1996, Montréal Canadiens players and fans marched down Sainte Catherine Street from the Forum to the team's new home, Molson Centre, a parade reminiscent of a religious procession. The Canadian Press.

complete with incense, in a Roman Catholic church or an Episcopal cathedral. One alumna wrote that the football team at the University of Southern California "achieves the status of religion," while members of its cheering squad, the Song Girls, functioned as high priestesses. Devotees, many with painted faces, tattoos, and outlandish costumes, are called "fans" at sporting events, while religious devotees tend to be labeled "fanatics." Both fans and fanatics resort to prayer, and many use devotional aids: phylacteries, Buddhist prayer beads (*malas*), or rosaries for religion; "Homer Hankies" in Minnesota or the "Terrible Towel" in Pittsburgh. A holy day (holiday) in religion might be the Hindu Diwali, the Jewish Yom Kippur, or the Eastern Orthodox Pascha; in sports, Opening Day for baseball or Super Bowl Sunday.[8]

A member of the victorious team kisses the Stanley Cup or the Lombardi Trophy after a Super Bowl win and then holds it aloft, much the way a priest might venerate and elevate a saint's relic or an Orthodox bishop kisses a holy icon.

Both sports and religion have authorities: a referee or umpire in sports; a bishop, guru, imam, or rabbi in religion. A higher authority might be invoked from time to time: a cardinal or even the pope himself in Catholicism; the commissioner in sports. Relics? A piece of the true cross of Jesus, for example, or an autographed baseball from the 1920s. A baseball card is not all that different in size and appearance from a mass card. Finally, both religion and sports have something akin to sainthood; in sports, it's called the Hall of Fame.

At times, the nomenclature overlaps. Football fans in general, and Pittsburgh Steelers fans in particular, will never forget the "Immaculate Reception," when, on December 23, 1972, Franco Harris, a rookie, caught a deflected pass from Terry Bradshaw to beat the Oakland Raiders. Three years and five days later, Roger Staubach launched a fifty-yard, last-second touchdown pass to beat the Minnesota Vikings. "I closed my eyes and said a Hail Mary," Staubach, a Roman Catholic, later told a reporter. That term, "Hail Mary," has entered the sports lexicon to connote a long-shot, desperate attempt to win the game.

Another way that sports has eclipsed traditional expressions of religion is in the realm of moral clarity and leadership. The rise of the Religious Right in the late 1970s, in defense of racial segregation in evangelical institutions, and its subsequent alignment with the far-right precincts of the Republican Party, has muted evangelicalism's once-robust prophetic voice, especially on issues of racial equality. Sports figures, by contrast—LeBron James, Emmanuel Sanders, Jrue Holiday, Clayton Kershaw, Stephen Curry, Lewis Brinson, Kyrie Irving, the entire 2020 Atlanta Dream basketball team, and many others—have been unequivocal in their advocacy for social justice, including the Black Lives Matter movement. Both the Milwaukee Bucks and the Milwaukee Brewers refused to play games following the shooting of Jason Blake, an African American, in Kenosha, Wisconsin. The Detroit Lions canceled an entire day of practice after the Blake shooting to conduct an hours-long team meeting about racism. "We're going to spread our message," Trey Flowers said. "We're going to do it as a team." Hockey players forced a pause during the 2020 Stanley Cup playoffs in order to express their views on systemic racism, and the overwhelmingly white league announced mandatory programs for diversity training. "We look forward to working with all voices of change to fight for equality and broaden access to the game we all love," Gary Bettman, the NHL commissioner, declared. Even the famously conservative owners of the National Football League have acknowledged the imperative of racial justice. In terms of his life as a professional athlete, Colin Kaepernick must surely be regarded as a martyr for his convictions. Americans once looked to religious leaders for moral direction, figures like Walter Rauschenbusch, Dorothy Day, Abraham Joshua Heschel, Malcolm X, Reinhold Niebuhr, and Martin Luther King Jr. Now, as often as not, moral leadership emanates from the world of sports.[9]

Gender also plays a role in understanding the emergence of sports as something akin to religion at the turn of the twenty-first century. The demographics of the sports-radio audience, to take one example, skew overwhelmingly male—80 to 90 percent—which makes the medium a boon to advertisers, but it also helps to explain the passion for sports in North America. The four major sports in North America—baseball, football, hockey, and basketball—are still preponderantly a male preserve. That is not to say that women haven't been playing these sports (except for football), and the level of women's play and competition is increasing all the time. But despite the extraordinary advances wrought by Title IX in advancing women's athletics, the four major sports are still overwhelmingly populated with men, both in terms of participants and fans, although women have recently been tapped as officials, coaches, and even general managers.[10]

Aside from anecdotal evidence—sports radio, cable sports shows, a glance at the stands—one way to make this point would be to compare men's and women's professional basketball, the one major sport where women have an analogue professional league. According to 2019 statistics, the annual revenue for the National Basketball Association (NBA) was $7.4 billion, as compared with $60 million for the Women's National Basketball Association (WNBA). Average attendance throughout the season was 18,000 for the NBA, 6,798 for the WNBA; average player salary for the NBA was $6.4 million as opposed to $71,635 for the WNBA. The telecast of the 2019 NBA finals attracted an average of 15.14 million viewers; the 2018 WNBA finals averaged 231,000 viewers.[11]

The affinity between men and sports in the late twentieth century might be attributed in part to cultural circumstances. Catalyzed by the publication of *The Feminine Mystique* by Betty Friedan in 1963, second-wave feminism touched off a revolution in social mores, from the boardroom to the bedroom. The women's movement brought radical changes in gender roles, economic expectations, sexual behavior, the composition of families, and language. In 1945, the number of American women in the labor force stood at 29 percent; by 1970 that number rose to 38 percent, to 46 percent in 1995, and 46.9 percent in 2018; in Canada, the number was slightly higher: 47.7 percent. Women have not been content to stay at home, and, despite the well-publicized glass ceiling, they have entered every arena of American life, from the military to the Supreme Court, from the picket lines to the corporate hierarchy.[12]

By no means have women achieved equality or parity with men in terms of pay or opportunity. Not at all. But as women have fought for equality and claimed their rightful place in society, some men have felt displaced, elbowed aside when considered for college admissions, jobs, or promotions. Many American males regard gender equality as a zero-sum proposition; feminism, by this logic, is disruptive, a threat to their own well-being, and many have reacted in inappropriate, even violent, ways. Add to that the various economic vicissitudes over the past half century—from the Arab Oil Embargo of the 1970s to the Great Recession of 2008 and, more recently, the coronavirus—many men, especially white men, feel beleaguered, that the world isn't fair.

This sense of confusion and dislocation has fostered many responses and analyses. *Iron John: A Book About Men*, published in 1990 by the poet Robert Bly, celebrated the soft-breasted male and sought to provide positive models of masculinity. More recently, Arlie Russell Hochschild, a sociologist, visited southern Louisiana in an attempt to understand those who affiliated with the Tea Party movement during the Obama administration. Aside from economic dislocation, Hochschild encountered uneasiness about masculinity. "It wasn't easy being a man," she heard. "It was an era of numerous subtle challenges to masculinity, it seemed. These days a woman didn't need a man for financial support, for procreation, even for the status of being married."[13]

Amid such uncertainty, sports, which bears at least a family resemblance to religion, provides a respite, an alternative universe to a world that seems unfair and out of balance. Sports, especially at the collegiate and professional level, may offer the closest thing we have to a meritocracy: If you're not good enough, you won't play. Even accounting for race, disparities of wealth, and segregation by gender, sports nevertheless offers, both literally and proverbially, something very close to a level playing field where all contestants compete on an equal footing.

In addition, what all major sports have in common since the eclipse of mob games during the age of industrialism are clear boundaries and precise delineations. The fields of play are geometrical, with straight lines and right angles, and the two exceptions have historical precedents: the rounded corners of a hockey rink (reminiscent of backyard ponds) and the irregular dimensions of outfield fences in baseball (reflecting the unknown frontier).

In sports, the rules may be complex, but they too are precise, accounting for every situation and contingency. Something is either in bounds or out of bounds, safe or out, fair or foul. Bill Veeck, one of the most colorful sports impresarios of the twentieth century, remarked that baseball "is almost the only orderly thing in a very unorderly world." The same observation could be expanded to team sports in general.[14]

The only thing that can disrupt this orderly universe is a misjudgment, something that is becoming increasingly rare with the expansion of video review. Nothing enrages a sports fan more than a bad call from an official, whose job is to act as an impartial judge and a benign authority figure. The official has no prerogative to be a judicial activist. He cannot hear mitigating arguments before rendering his judgment. A batter thrown out by a step at first base, for example, cannot argue that he should be called safe because, had he not injured his ankle back in spring training, he would almost certainly have beaten the throw from shortstop and that to call him out on that play betrayed the umpire's bias against players who are in some way disabled. The wide receiver who failed to plant both feet in bounds before falling out of the end zone cannot argue that he simply forgot to do so and that such negligence should not be held against him and that, furthermore, any adverse ruling would unfairly punish the entire team for the inadvertent lapse of one of its players. No, the officials must render simple, impartial judgments lest they violate the orderly universe that is the world of sports. As Veeck said, "If you get three strikes, even the best lawyer in the world can't get you off."[15]

It is a world seemingly at odds with the real world. Therein lies its appeal. "Sports is the ultimate escapism vehicle," according to Chris Oliviero of CBS Radio. "No matter what's going on in somebody's life, they can take three hours to watch a game on Sunday and get away from all the negativity in the world." He added, "It gives people that vehicle to just be a fan." Sports provides the safety of a subculture, a place of refuge from the broader world. It may not in fact be an *ideal* world, but it is certainly an *idealized* world.[16]

Even so, however, the real world has a way of intruding into the realm of sports. Issues of race and gender and, more recently, transgender identity provoke comment, reflection, and reaction. Economics and economic inequality always loom. Patriotism and the peculiar custom of singing national anthems before sporting events—and not at, say, rock concerts or a museum opening or a motion picture premiere—go unquestioned, until the custom is challenged, or its meaning reconfigured. Anyone determined to mount such a challenge, however—Mahmoud Abdul-Rauf or Colin Kaepernick come to mind—faces the obloquy of teammates, fans, and owners and even the end of one's professional career. When Jim "Mudcat" Grant, pitcher for the Cleveland Indians, improvised the final measures of *The Star-Spangled Banner* in September 1960—"This land is not so free, I can't even go to Mississippi"—he was suspended without pay for the remainder of the season.[17]

The world of sports, like the world of religion, is not without controversy. But despite these intrusions, for many the lure of an alternative universe remains strong, even irresistible, affording both escape and a sense of community. Anticipating his return to the ballpark after a season of exclusion because of the coronavirus, a Nationals fan told the *Washington Post*, "It's entering a different world of familiar pleasures, rituals, excitement, companionship, with an outcome."[18]

For an older generation of American males, military service in World War II or the Korean War provided the venue for bonding with other men. Strong ties of friendship and camaraderie were forged in bunkers,

in air squadrons, or onboard a destroyer. Many in the succeeding generation sought to avoid the draft, so they have no regiment reunions to show
for their friendships; they do not gather in VFW halls to swap war stories
and renew ties with their combat buddies.

The stories of subsequent generations are stories of athletic prowess: the improbable touchdown pass, the hat trick or the no-hitter, Stephen Curry's magnificent arc from mid-court, Matthew Stafford's latest
fourth-quarter comeback. The interest in sports and sports memorabilia
almost certainly connotes a nostalgia for the simpler days of childhood,
but it also provides a common vocabulary for male interaction and bonding. This is the language of the disaffected male and the foundation of a
powerful new impulse, one that inspires uncommon devotion.

Any relationship has its share of paradoxes, and the almost symbiotic
connection between white men and team sports is no exception. First,
there are economic anomalies: the struggling blue-collar worker cheering for players who make more in a single season than the worker might
earn in the course of his lifetime.

Second, the paradox of white fans watching and appreciating the athleticism of players, many of whom are not white. This could be entirely
innocent and race-blind, but it could also reflect a systemic and race-based
assumption that the appropriate arena of self-expression for Black people
and other people of color is, well, the arena and not so much the world
outside the stadium. This sort of racism, though it may not be acknowledged as such by white fans, might explain the white backlash against
Kaepernick and other players who kneeled during the national anthem;
so long as they are considered mascots—or gladiators—competing
within the confines of the game itself, they are worthy of respect, even
adulation, but once they dare to express themselves on matters beyond
sports, they are vilified and ostracized. In a narrow sense, that response
might be expected, even understandable; having fled the real world into
a parallel universe of clear expectations and tidy boundaries, white fans
are loath to be reminded of what they seek to ignore, and so they punish
athletes of color who dare to erase an idealized separation between sports
and politics. In 1961, after Bill Russell, star of the Boston Celtics, led a
walkout of Black players from an NBA game in Lexington, Kentucky, to

protest racial discrimination, he said, "I am coming to the realization that we are accepted as entertainers, but that we are not accepted as people in some places."[19]

Perhaps no one better illustrates this racial double standard than Laura Ingraham, Fox television personality. When Drew Brees, quarterback for the New Orleans Saints, who is white, declared that he "will never agree" with NFL players who kneel during the national anthem, Ingraham said, "He's allowed to have his view," and added, "He's a person, he has some worth." Earlier, however, when Black NBA players LeBron James and Kevin Durant expressed support for the Black Lives Matter movement, Ingraham instructed them to "keep the political commentary to yourself" and "shut up and dribble."[20]

This bifurcation manifests itself on both sides of the political spectrum. Boston Red Sox fans hailed Curt Schilling's heroic efforts to bring the city a championship in 2004, ending an eighty-six-year drought. But Schilling's hard-right sympathies—comparing Muslims to Nazis, suggesting that journalists should be lynched or that Hillary Clinton "should be buried under a jail somewhere," belittling transgender rights—cost him an analyst position with ESPN and, very likely, election to the Hall of Fame.[21]

This treating of athletes differently on and off the field may be nothing new. Whereas ancient Greeks valorized athletes and actors, Rome regarded them as negligible, even dishonorable. Tertullian, the early church father who lived at the turn of the third century, commented on contemporary spectacles and what he characterized as the "perversity" of popular attitudes toward the players. "The characters and actors of these spectacles, the charioteers, stage heroes, boxers and gladiators of which people are so fond, to whom men submit their souls and women even submit their bodies," he wrote, "are at the same time both despised and exalted; they are even condemned to infamy and denied the rights of citizens."[22]

The racial divide in contemporary sports, however, cannot be ignored in accounting for the chasm between adulation and opprobrium. The specter of white male fans cheering for athletes of color in the arena may be nothing more than that—spectators appreciating the beauty of the game, physical prowess, and the thrill of competition. But another, nefarious interpretation cannot be dismissed altogether, and it may even coexist with that benign view. It is suggested to me by the harrowing scene in the opening chapter of Ralph's Ellison's novel *Invisible Man*, where Black teenagers, blindfolded, were herded into a boxing ring to pummel one another for the amusement of tuxedoed male spectators in a smoke-filled ballroom. Then, exhausted, glistening with sweat, and on hands and knees, they were forced to collect their compensation—coins and worthless brass tokens interspersed with a few crumpled dollar bills—from an electrified carpet, once again for the merriment of the crowd.[23]

Parallels with the contemporary world of sports, thankfully, are not exact, but I'm struck by white men posing as something akin to overlords of the athletic arena—how many professional team owners are *not* white?—but this may apply to fandom as well. In this alternate universe of sports, athletes, especially athletes of color, are expected to "stay in their lane" and forbear speaking out on matters other than sports, as Bill Russell attested, and Colin Kaepernick learned. And to add a gender component to this analysis, where are women in this hyper-masculinized universe? If they appear at all, they typically are relegated—literally—to the sidelines as cheerleaders or "ball girls." I can't claim any experience or much knowledge of fantasy sports, but it appears that allowing fans to pose as general managers and assemble fantasy teams carries with it the corollary of viewing athletes as commodities, a form of chattel expected to perform, not opine.

Shut up and dribble.

The final paradox surrounding this affinity between white fans and sports is that a white male demographic putatively devoted to rugged individualism has gravitated to *team* sports, suggesting that the fundamental lure of community, once satisfied by religious affiliation, has migrated to a secular venue: the stadium or its virtual counterpart, sports radio.[24]

Clearly, the passion for team sports is fulfilling some need in contemporary society—the search for escape or community or transcendence. In many ways, sports supersedes religion in twenty-first-century North America. It invites our allegiance and devotion. It is susceptible to charismatic personalities. Like religion, sports is capable of social amelioration (racial desegregation) as well as great harm (violence and injury). Above all, like religion, the world of sports provides an orderly universe, one insulated from the vicissitudes and the dysfunction of the larger world. "Baseball is better than life," Robert DeNiro's character says in the 1996 film *The Fan*. "It's fair." At a time when many people perceive the world as unfair—economic inequality, preferential treatment for others based on race or gender or sexual orientation—sports offers an alternative world, one where the rules are unambiguous and impartially enforced. Sports does not perfectly appropriate the platonic ideal of fairness, of course, but for many it comes much closer than the real world.[25]

The notion of sports as analogous to religion may help to explain its popularity. Americans are still a traditionally religious people, but increasingly less so; at the same time, we are becoming more and more invested in organized sports—*invested* in every sense of the word. Just as religion diverts our attention from this-worldly matters to the transcendent, so too sports allows us to set aside our quotidian concerns, even if only for a few hours. Therein lies at least part of its appeal.

This is why, circling back to Tom Brady and the underinflated footballs, cheating matters. In an age of moral relativism and growing religious indifference—when, for example, a president issues well over thirty thousand false or misleading statements in the course of his four-year term, or his spokesperson brags about employing "alternative facts"—sports provides something very close to fixed moral standards. Setting aside whether or not the New England Patriots actually engaged in chicanery (still a matter of contestation), cheating, or even the prospect of cheating, violates not only integrity of the game, it also ruptures the orderly universe of sports. The electronic sign-stealing by the Houston Astros in 2017 and 2018 provides another case in point. Even the commissioner of Major League Baseball underestimated the outrage of fans and players over this brazen violation of the rules and breach of protocol. When Rob Manfred, the commissioner, defended his decision not to strip the Astros of their championship by referring to the trophy as a "piece of metal," he further enraged the aggrieved parties—those whose allegiance presupposes the absolute integrity of the sport.[26]

The world of sports provides the shelter of a subculture, a contrived universe with its own standards, rules, and values—its own heroes and villains, rituals and sacred spaces. It is a place where, in contrast to the larger culture, rules are clear and impartially enforced. At its best, it approximates a perfect meritocracy. Amid a world perceived as disordered and unfair, this universe—this religion—provides shelter, a common vocabulary, shared assumptions, and the assurance of camaraderie.

It's a wonderful, enchanted universe.

ACKNOWLEDGMENTS

A book decades in the making accrues a lot of debts.

I can forgive my colleagues at Dartmouth College for suspecting that my "sports book" was an illusion, in part because it represents something of a departure from my previous scholarship. I nevertheless appreciate their support. The Leslie Center for the Humanities provided financial assistance for travel costs and to purchase rights for illustrations, and the dean's office supplied a subvention for the illustrations. In addition, Dartmouth has a wonderful program in which undergraduates sign on as research assistants. Two of these Presidential Scholars, Christopher Huberty and Jack Heneghan, contributed valuable research during the early stages of this project.

During the summer of 2019, I presented some of these ideas at the Congregational Summer Assembly, in Frankfort, Michigan. This was the second time I had been honored to give the George M. Gibson Lectures there. At the end of the week, I left fearing that some of the material I presented had been a bit too inchoate, but I'm grateful for both the opportunity and the feedback.

The coronavirus pandemic limited some of the archival research I had planned, so I appreciate help from afar. I'm especially grateful to Cassidy Lent at the Baseball Hall of Fame, in Cooperstown, New York, for her assistance during my visit there.

Elaine Maisner and John Sherer at the University of North Carolina Press have been enthusiastic about this project from the beginning. I appreciate their unstinting support, astute guidance, and encouragement. Thanks also to their superb staff, including Andreina Fernandez, Erin Granville, Matthew Somoroff, and Lindsay Starr, for shepherding the manuscript to publication. For years, friends and colleagues have urged me to secure the services of a literary agent. Having had two bad experiences several decades apart, I resisted, but Carol Mann and her eponymous agency changed my thinking. Thank you.

Sean Griffin, an extraordinary scholar, came to Dartmouth in 2017 under the auspices of the Society of Fellows, which I directed at the time. He is also a sports fan and a good friend who reviewed the manuscript and offered helpful suggestions, especially on the basketball chapter. Bernie Van De Walle, a long-ago former student, provided similar assistance on the hockey chapter. Edward Blum read an early draft on the manuscript and offered his usual incisive comments, and Jeffrey Scholes provided similar assistance on the penultimate draft. My friend Robert Oden, president emeritus of Carleton College, has encouraged this project from the beginning. He also carefully read this manuscript, which benefited considerably from his attention.

I wrote in the introduction that the immediate catalyst for this book was my introduction to sports radio in the 1990s. That is certainly the case, although it doesn't tell the whole story. I've been blessed with several wonderful mentors over the years, but John Murrin at Princeton University started me thinking about sports in a new way. He was a stalwart member of the History Department intramural softball team, which he named the Revolting Masses purely for the satisfaction of hearing members of the Princeton administration—putatively more conservative than the rest of us—chant the customary tribute to the opposing team following a game: "Rah, rah, rah, Revolting Masses!" (One of the highlights of my doctoral studies at Princeton was being asked to coach the Revolting Masses, although I've yet to figure out a way to include that on my CV.)

I've often said that John Murrin forgot more about colonial history than most of us in the field would ever know, but his incomparable intellect ranged far and wide. Very often his conversations would veer into sports, one of his true loves, and he would talk about some of the ideas I've tried to develop here: baseball as immigrant game, football as military game, basketball as urban game. (I don't recall him ever talking about hockey, so if my chapter on hockey doesn't measure up to the others, that's probably why.)

Over the ensuing decades, I've played with these ideas, and I'd like to believe that I expanded them somewhat, especially the dimensions of religion, gender, and race. But I also want to be clear that John deserves the credit, and I would gladly have deferred to him in the writing of a book about team sports in North America. This book is gratefully dedicated to John and his equally remarkable wife, Mary.

Sadly, John did not live to see this book; he succumbed to the coronavirus in 2020. What I wouldn't have given once again to have him cast his critical eyes on something I had written. He was an extraordinary man, without a doubt one of the formative influences on my life. I miss him.

Finally, my greatest debt, as always, is to my wife, the estimable Catharine Randall, without whom . . .

NOTES

INTRODUCTION

1. "Jerome from Manhattan," as he was known to listeners, was Jerome Mittelman; see John Freeman Gill, "Seventh-Inning Kvetch," *New York Times*, October 24, 2004, sect. 14, 4. Other sports radio markets also have their regular callers; see, for example, Randy Peterson, "'Tommy from Des Moines' Dies: Central Iowa Talk Radio—and Coaches at Iowa State and Iowa—Will Miss Him," *Des Moines Register*, December 6, 2019.

2. Benjamin Hochman, "From Hy-Vee to the Hall—Taking Stock of Warner's Rise," *St. Louis Post-Dispatch*, August 6, 2017; Helene Elliott, "David Ayres Achieves the Dream Thanks to One of Hockey's Quirks," *Los Angeles Times*, February 29, 2020; James Wagner, "Called Back Up to the Majors, 12 Years Later," *New York Times*, April 18, 2021, D5. On sports as religion, see, for example, Brad Schultz and Mary Lou Sheffer, eds., *Sport and Religion in the Twenty-First Century* (Lanham, Md.: Lexington Books, 2016).

3. On Muscular Christianity, see William E. Winn, "Tom Brown's Schooldays and the Development of 'Muscular Christianity,'" *Church History* 29, no. 1 (March 1960): 64–73; Clifford Putney, *Muscular Christianity: Manhood and Sports in Protestant America, 1880–1920* (Cambridge, Mass.: Harvard University Press, 2001); Paul W. Bennett, "Training 'Blue-Blooded' Canadian Boys: Athleticism, Muscular Christianity, and Sports in Ontario's 'Little Big Four' Schools, 1829–1930," *Journal of Sports History* 43, no. 3 (Fall 2016): 253–71. For an example of the enduring popularity of athletic metaphors in Christianity, see Gordon MacDonald, *A Resilient Life: You Can Move Ahead No Matter What* (Nashville: Thomas Nelson, 2004).

4. See, for example, Timothy B. Neary, *Crossing Parish Boundaries: Race, Sports, and Catholic Youth in Chicago, 1914–1954* (Chicago: University of Chicago Press, 2016); Julie Byrne, *O God of Players: The Story of the Immaculata Mighty Macs* (New York: Columbia University Press, 2003); Benjamin Rabinowitz, "The Young Men's Hebrew Associations (1854–1913)," *Publications*

of the American Jewish Historical Society, no. 37 (1947): 221–326; Linda J. Borish, "'An Interest in Physical Well-Being among the Feminine Membership': Sporting Activities for Women at Young Men's and Young Women's Hebrew Associations," *American Jewish History* 87, no. 1 (March 1999): 61–93.

5. Frank Deford, "Religion in Sport," *Sports Illustrated*, April 19, 1976.

6. Quoted in Frank Deford, "A Gentleman and a Scholar," *Sports Illustrated*, April 17, 1989, 98.

7. Garrison Keillor characterizes soccer as "recreational milling" more than organized sport; *That Time of Year: A Minnesota Life* (New York: Arcade Publishing, 2020), 202. On the costs of hockey, see Étienne Lajoie and Salim Valji, "In Canada, the Cost of Youth Hockey Benches the Next Generation," *New York Times*, February 24, 2020; Bruce Berglund, *The Fastest Game in the World: Hockey and the Globalization of Sports* (Oakland: University of California Press, 2021), 17.

8. Regarding "sporting congregations," see Derrick E. White, *Blood, Sweat, and Tears: Jake Gaither, Florida A&M, and the History of Black College Football* (Chapel Hill: University of North Carolina Press, 2019), chap. 1.

CHAPTER 1

1. The account of Jesus writing in the sand is found in John 8:1–11. Because this Cooperstown account is mythical, some of the details vary as the story has been recounted over the years.

2. On the Doubleday myth, see Thomas L. Altherr, "Abner Doubleday and the 'Invention' of Baseball," in *Replays, Rivalries, and Rumbles: The Most Iconic Moments in American Sports*, ed. Steven Gietschier (Urbana and Chicago: University of Illinois Press, 2017), 1–9; Christopher H. Evans, "Baseball as Civil Religion: The Genesis of an American Creation Story," in *The Faith of Fifty Million: Baseball, Religion, and American Culture*, ed. Christopher H. Evans and William R. Herzog II (Louisville: Westminster John Knox Press, 2002), chap. 1; cf. Stephen Jay Gould, *Triumph and Tragedy in Mudville: A Lifelong Passion for Baseball* (New York: W. W. Norton, 2003), 190–204. Stephen Clark was the brother of Robert Sterling Clark, an art collector whose collection formed the core of the Clark Art Museum in Williamstown, Massachusetts; see Nicholas Niarchos, "Sensorial Supper," *New Yorker*, May 13, 2019, 16. The brothers were heirs to the Singer sewing-machine fortune.

3. Quoted in "History of the Museum," National Baseball Hall of Fame (website), accessed April 6, 2019, https://baseballhall.org/about-the-hall.

4. For a biographical sketch of Doubleday and his relationship with Albert G. Spalding, see David Block, *Baseball before We Knew It: A Search for the Roots*

of the Game (Lincoln: University of Nebraska Press, 2005), chap. 3. A variation on the Doubleday myth is that Doubleday, while heading the Freedmen's Bureau in Galveston County, Texas, introduced baseball to Texas in 1867; see John M. Carroll, "The Doubleday Myth and Texas Baseball," *Southwestern Historical Quarterly* 92, no. 4 (April 1989): 596–612.

5. Quoted in Monica Nucciarone, *Alexander Cartwright: The Life behind the Baseball Legend* (Lincoln: University of Nebraska Press, 2009), xxv. On baseball's world tour, see Mark Lamster, *Spalding's World Tour: The Epic Adventure That Took Baseball Around the World—and Made It America's Game* (New York: PublicAffairs, 2006). Lamster renders Twain's quote slightly differently (xvi).

6. James Mallinson, "A. G. Mills," Society for American Baseball Research, accessed April 6, 2019, https://sabr.org/bioproj/person/abccef1b; quoted in John Thorn, *Baseball in the Garden of Eden: The Secret History of the Early Game* (New York: Simon & Schuster, 2011), 11.

7. Quoted in Thorn, *Baseball in the Garden of Eden*, 5. The quest to identify the origins of baseball is not unlike the recent mania in American jurisprudence to divine the "original intent" of the founders.

8. "Abner Graves Identifies Abner Doubleday as the 'Father of Baseball,'" in *Early Innings: A Documentary History of Baseball, 1825–1908*, ed. Dean A. Sullivan (Lincoln: University of Nebraska Press, 1995), 285; Block, *Baseball before We Knew It*, 52, 55–56.

9. "Final Decision of the Special Base Ball Commission," in Sullivan, *Early Innings*, 293–95, passim. Graves's letters are reproduced as appendix 4 in Block, *Baseball before We Knew It*, 252–56.

10. Quoted in Thorn, *Baseball in the Garden of Eden*, 17–18.

11. *A Little Pretty Pocket Book* (London: J Newbery, 1744), n.p. The publisher, John Newbery, is the namesake for the Newbery Medal, awarded for "the most distinguished contribution to American literature for children" ("John Newbery Medal," Association for Library Service to Children, American Library Association, accessed December 30, 2021, www.ala.org/alsc/awardsgrants/bookmedia/newbery).

12. Frank Litsky, "Now Pittsfield Stakes Claim to Baseball's Origins," *New York Times*, May 12, 2004. The mention of "Football" in the document is almost certainly a reference to what Americans now call soccer.

13. William Croswell, letter drafted to the Harvard Corporation, December 1827, Papers of William Croswell [Call number HUG 1306.5], Harvard University Archives; Samuel Longfellow, ed., *Life of Henry Wadsworth Longfellow with Extracts from His Journals and Correspondence* (Boston: Ticknor, 1886), 1:51; Frank Presbrey and James Hugh Moffatt, eds., *Athletics at Princeton: A History* (New York: Frank Presbrey Co., 1901), 67; *Pittsfield Sun*, July 7, 1859;

Samuel R. Hill, "Baseball in Canada," *Indiana Journal of Global Legal Studies* 8, no. 1 (Fall 2000): 44. For baseball in Canada, see also William Humber, *Diamonds of the North: A Concise History of Baseball in Canada* (Toronto: Oxford University Press, 1995).

14. John King Lord, *A History of Dartmouth College, 1815–1909* (Concord, N.H.: Rumford Press, 1913), 564; *Indiana Journal*, May 13, 1837.

15. Cleveland City Council Archives, March 4, 1845.

16. "A Defense of Baseball as a 'Manly Exercise' (1856)," in Sullivan, *Early Innings*, 21.

17. Walt Whitman, "City Intelligence," *Brooklyn Daily Eagle*, July 23, 1846. On Whitman and baseball, see Lowell Edwin Folsom, "America's 'Hurrah Game': Baseball and Walt Whitman," *Iowa Review* 11, no. 2/3 (Spring/Summer 1980): 68–80.

18. Goldstein, *Playing for Keeps*, 25; quoted in Benjamin G. Rader, *Baseball: A History of America's Game* (Urbana: University of Illinois Press, 2002), 10; quoted in Thomas L. Altherr, "'The Most Summery, Bold, Free & Spacious Game': Charles King Newcomb and Philadelphia Baseball, 1866–1871," *Pennsylvania History: A Journal of Mid-Atlantic Studies* 52, no. 2 (April 1985): 75.

19. Quoted in Altherr, "'Most Summery, Bold, Free & Spacious Game,'" 74.

20. Albert G. Spalding, "Why Base Ball Has Become Our National Game," in *Great American Baseball Stories*, ed. Jeff Silverman (Guilford, Conn.: Lyons Press, 2019), 6; Horace Greeley, *Recollections of a Busy Life* (New York: J. B. Ford, 1869), 117; Harriet Raymond Lloyd, ed., *Life and Letters of John Howard Raymond, Late President of Vassar College* (New York: Ford, Howard & Hulbert, 1881), 38; Henry Chadwick, "The Model Base Ball Player," in Silverman, *Great American Baseball Stories*, 15.

21. The Massachusetts game rules appear in Sullivan, *Early Innings*, 15–16. The rule about hitting the runner between bases is rule 14.

22. Block, *Baseball before We Knew It*, chap. 6, quote on 91. Regarding the first game, see Melvin L. Adelman, "The First Baseball Game, the First Newspaper References to Baseball, and the New York Club: A Note on the Early History of Baseball," *Journal of Sport History* 7, no. 3 (Winter 1980): 132–35.

23. Much of this biographical information comes from Nucciarone, *Alexander Cartwright*, chaps. 1–2, quote on 21; Warren Goldstein, *Playing for Keeps: A History of Early Baseball* (Ithaca, N.Y.: Cornell University Press, 1989), 12. On Cartwright, see also Jay Martin, *Live All You Can: Alexander Joy Cartwright and the Invention of Modern Baseball* (New York: Columbia University Press, 2009).

24. Humber, *Diamonds of the North*, 4; Patrick B. Miller, "The Manly, the Moral, and the Proficient: College Sport in the New South," *Journal of Sport History* 24, no. 3 (Fall 1997): 291; Robert Gudmestad, "Baseball, the Lost

Cause, and the New South in Richmond, Virginia," in *The Sporting World of the Modern South*, ed. Patrick B. Miller (Urbana: University of Illinois Press, 2002), 52–80. On baseball during the Civil War, see George B. Kirsch, *Baseball in Blue and Gray: The National Pastime during the Civil War* (Princeton, N.J.: Princeton University Press, 2003).

25. Quoted in Joseph L. Price, *Rounding the Bases: Baseball and Religion in America* (Macon, Ga.: Mercer University Press, 2006), 130; George F. Will, *Men at Work: The Craft of Baseball* (New York: Macmillan, 1990), 328.

26. Rader, *Baseball*, 9–10; "The Incoming Base Ball Season," in Sullivan, *Early Innings*, 45–46. On the construction of Fenway Park, see Glenn Stout, *Fenway 1912: The Birth of a Ballpark, a Championship Season, and Fenway's Remarkable First Year* (Boston: Mariner Books, 2011).

27. Philip Roth, "My Baseball Years," *Reading Myself and Others* (New York: Farrar, Straus and Giroux, 1975), 181; Tom Stanton, *The Final Season: Fathers, Sons, and One Last Season in a Classic American Ballpark* (New York: St. Martin's Press, 2001), 13–14.

28. On the enduring appeal of baseball in rural areas, see David Vaught, "Abner Doubleday, Marc Bloch, and the Cultural Significance of Baseball in Rural America," *Agricultural History* 85, no. 1 (Winter 2011): 1–20; John Mihelich, "'Baseball Was Our Life': Amateur Baseball in Butte, Montana, 1920–1960," *Montana Historical Quarterly* 59, no. 2 (Summer 2009): 62–72, 96.

29. A. Bartlett Giamatti, *A Great and Glorious Game: Baseball Writings of A. Bartlett Giamatti*, ed. Kenneth S. Robson (Chapel Hill, N.C.: Algonquin Books, 1998), 8.

30. "The Incoming Base Ball Season," in Sullivan, *Early Innings*, 47; "The Widespread Popularity of Baseball (1888)," in Sullivan, *Early Innings*, 157.

31. Michael Mandelbaum, *The Meaning of Sports: Why Americans Watch Baseball, Football, and Basketball and What They See When They Do* (New York: Public Affairs, 2004), 41; Giamatti, *Great and Glorious Game*, 7.

32. Under pressure, the Red Sox had reluctantly given Jackie Robinson and two other African Americans a tryout in 1945. The team refused to sign any of the players. See Glenn Stout, "Tryout and Fallout: Race, Jackie Robinson, and the Red Sox," *Massachusetts Historical Review*, 6 (2004): 11–37.

33. Benjamin Hoffman, "Before Robinson, There Was Fowler," *New York Times*, December 7, 2021, B7 (Fowler was elected to the Hall of Fame in 2021); Jeffrey Powers-Beck, "'Chief': The American Indian Integration of Baseball, 1897–1945," *American Indian Quarterly* 25, no. 4 (Autumn 2001): 508–38, quotes on 526, 511. After the Cleveland Indians name was announced on January 16, 1915, the *Cleveland Plain Dealer* remarked that the team's new name "also serves to revive the memory of a single great player": Sockalexis.

34. Price, *Rounding the Bases,* chap. 2; Jim Warnock, "The Mormon Game: The Religious Uses of Baseball in Early Utah," *Nine: A Journal of Baseball History and Social Policy Perspectives* 6, no. 1 (Fall 1997): 1–14; Stephen H. Norwood and Harold Brackman, "Going to Bat for Jackie Robinson: The Jewish Role in Breaking Baseball's Color Line," *Journal of Sport History* 26, no. 1 (Spring 1999): 115–141, quote on 128. On Greenberg, see Mark Kurlansky, *Hank Greenberg: The Hero Who Didn't Want to Be One* (New Haven, Conn.: Yale University Press, 2011); Hank Greenberg, *The Story of My Life,* ed. Ira Berkow (Chicago: Ivan R. Dee, 1989).

35. David K. Wiggins, "Wendell Smith, the *Pittsburgh Courier-Journal* and the Campaign to Include Blacks in Organized Baseball, 1933–1945," *Journal of Sport History* 10, no. 2 (Summer 1983): 7.

36. Norwood and Brackman, "Going to Bat for Jackie Robinson"; Chris Lamb, "'I Never Want to Take Another Trip Like This One': Jackie Robinson's Journey to Integrate Baseball," *Journal of Sport History* 24, no. 2 (Summer 1997), 178; Wiggins, "Wendell Smith"; Arnold Rampersad, *Jackie Robinson: A Biography* (New York: Random House, 1997), 119–29, quote on 167; in his autobiography, Robinson credited Smith for giving Robinson the opportunity (see Rampersad, 5).

37. On Robinson, see Rampersad, *Jackie Robinson*; Jules Tygiel, *Baseball's Great Experiment: Jackie Robinson and His Legacy* (New York: Oxford University Press, 1983); Roger Kahn, *Rickey & Robinson: The True, Untold Story of the Integration of Baseball* (New York: Rodale, 2014). On the newest immigrants excelling in baseball, see James Wagner, "'We All Know Where We Came From,'" *New York Times,* October 6, 2021.

38. Gould, *Triumph and Tragedy,* 30; quoted in George Cantor, *The Tigers of '68: Baseball's Last Real Champions* (Dallas, Tex.: Taylor, 1997), 161.

39. Roth, "My Baseball Years," 181. For an example of the role of immigrants in the early years of professional baseball, see Edward Achorn, *The Summer of Beer and Whiskey: How Brewers, Barkeeps, Rowdies, Immigrants, and a Wild Pennant Fight Made Baseball America's Game* (New York: PublicAffairs, 2013).

40. Phil Alden Robinson, *Field of Dreams* screenplay (1988), p. 102, www.dailyscript.com/scripts/Field_of_Dreams.pdf.

41. Price, *Rounding the Bases,* chap. 3; John Sexton, *Baseball as a Road to God: Seeing Beyond the Game* (New York: Gotham Books, 2013).

42. Helen Tworkov, "The Baseball Diamond Sutra," *Tricycle: The Buddhist Review,* 2/3 (Summer 1993): 4. One scholar who takes a more tongue-in-cheek approach to this matter is Donald Lopez Jr., *Buddha Takes the Mound:*

Enlightenment in 9 Innings (New York: St. Martin's, 2020). He creatively uses baseball as a way of explaining Buddhism.

43. Thomas Boswell, *Why Time Begins on Opening Day* (New York: Penguin), 1985. The dead-ball era lasted from about 1900 to 1919; Murderers' Row was the moniker attached to the New York Yankees' power-hitting lineup in the late 1920s; the Big Red Machine refers to the dominance of the Cincinnati Reds during the 1970s.

44. Robinson, *Field of Dreams*, 102.

CHAPTER 2

1. "Colleges Deplore Games for Profit," *New York Times*, December 31, 1925.

2. Quoted in Ronald A. Smith, *Sports and Freedom: The Rise of Big-Time College Athletics* (New York: Oxford University Press, 1988), 74.

3. George E. Merrill, "Is Football Good Sport?" *North American Review*, 17 (November 1903): 764; Charles W. Eliot, "College Football," *Journal of Education*, 61 (February 16, 1905): 171–72; "No Mollycoddles, Says Roosevelt," *New York Times*, February 24, 1907.

4. "No Foes to Football: St. Andrew Brotherhood Tacitly Indorsed Great Game," *Washington Post*, October 1, 1898, 7.

5. J. William White and Horatio C. Wood, "Intercollegiate Football," *North American Review*, 158 (January 1894): 102; Oliver S. Jones, "Morality in College Athletics," *North American Review*, 160 (May 1895): 638–40; John Franklin Cowell, *Personal Reflections of Trinity College, North Carolina, 1887–1894* (Durham, N.C.: Duke University Press, 1939), 225; "The Value of the Game," *Boston Globe*, December 28, 1894; Charles F. Thwing, "Football a Game of Brains," *Independent* (New York City), December 10, 1891, 1; "Football Promotes Morals," *New York Times*, December 8, 1907.

6. "President Patton of Princeton on Football," *Hartford Courant*, November 16, 1898; Henry S. Curtis, "Football," *Journal of Education*, 84 (October 1916): 382.

7. Christopher Rowley, *The Shared Origins of Football, Rugby, and Soccer* (Lanham, Md.: Rowman & Littlefield, 2015), 65.

8. Rowley, *Shared Origins*, 94, 112. Regarding Ellis, see William J. Baker, "William Webb Ellis and the Origins of Rugby Football: The Life and Death of a Victorian Myth," *Albion: A Quarterly Journal Concerned with British Studies* 13, no. 2 (Summer 1981): 117–30. Ellis became an Anglican clergyman; his statue stands outside Rugby School, and his name is emblazoned on the Rugby World Cup.

9. Rowley, *Shared Origins*, 129–30.

10. John Langdon Sibley, "The Football Burial Services in 1860," in *The First Crusade against Football: Injuries, Brutality and Death in American Football from Bloody Monday to the Flying Wedge* (Ventura, Calif.: Lost Century of Sports Collection, 2017), 27–30; "Harvard Magazine," in *First Crusade against Football*, 26.

11. Rowley, *Shared Origins*, 130–31.

12. "The First Game: Nov. 6, 1869," https://scarletknights.com/sports/2017/6/11/sports-m-footbl-archive-first-game-html.aspx; "Paralysis Fatal to Dr. Leggett," *Central New Jersey Home News*, October 29, 1925, 1; David W. Major, "It Happened Here First," *Rutgers Magazine*, Fall 2019.

13. Rowley, *Shared Origins*, 133–34; quoted in Char Miller, *Gifford Pinchot and the Making of Modern Environmentalism* (Washington, D.C.: Island Press, 2001), 47.

14. Rowley, *Shared Origins*, 137.

15. Rowley, *Shared Origins*, 138.

16. Elliott J. Gorn and Warren Goldstein, *A Brief History of American Sports*, 2nd ed. (Urbana: University of Illinois Press, 1993), 158.

17. "Morals of Football: Walter Camp Tells How Much It Does for Youth," *Baltimore Sun*, December 23, 1907, 10.

18. Rowley, *Shared Origins*, 139–40.

19. Gorn and Goldstein, *Brief History of American Sports*, 157; Harford Powel Jr., "Walter Camp," *Youth's Companion*, September 23, 1926, 683; "To Kill Football Bill: Gov. Atkinson Will Veto the Prohibitive Measure," *Washington Post*, December 6, 1897; Christopher C. Meyers, "'Unrelenting War on Football': The Death of Richard Von Gammon and the Attempt to Ban Football in Georgia," *Georgia Historical Quarterly* 93, no. 4 (Winter 2009): 388–407.

20. Walter Camp, *The Book of Foot-ball* (New York: Century Co., 1910), 257, 192, 195, 202, 211; "Walter Camp," in *First Crusade against Football*, 107; "Walter Camp Reports on the First Army-Navy Game," *Outing Magazine*, November 1891.

21. "Is Football a Dangerous Sport?" in *First Crusade against Football*, 106.

22. Charles F. Thwing, "Football a Game of Brains," *Independent*, December 10, 1891; quoted in Ron Fimrite, "Once Powerful, Still Proud," *Sports Illustrated*, October 14, 1996, 8; quoted in Scott A. McQuilken and Ronald A. Smith, "The Rise and Fall of the Flying Wedge: Football's Most Controversial Play," *Journal of Sport History* 20, no. 1 (Spring 1993): 59.

23. Charles D. Daly, "Our Greatest Fighting Game," *Leslie's Illustrated Weekly*, October 22, 1921, 532; Camp, *Book of Foot-ball*, 159.

24. Daly, "Our Greatest Fighting Game," 533; Charles D. Daly, *American Football* (New York: Harper & Brothers, 1921), 1, 4, 32, 59.

25. Daly, *American Football*, 148.

26. "*The Boston Daily Globe*," in *First Crusade against Football*, 122.

27. "*The Boston Daily Globe*," in *First Crusade against Football*, 123; McQuilken and Smith, "Rise and Fall of the Flying Wedge," 57–64. Deland signed on as an adviser to the Harvard football team in 1892 and was the team's head coach for three games in 1895.

28. Rules against some form of the flying wedge are periodically updated to thwart the ingenuity of coaches who persist in finding ways to employ it. See Jonathan Chait, "College Football Bans Wedge Blocking on Kickoffs," *New Republic*, April 16, 2010.

29. Steven W. Pope, "An Army of Athletes: Playing Fields, Battlefields, and the American Military Experience, 1890–1920," *Journal of Military History* 59, no. 3 (July 1995): 435–56; quotes on 440, 448.

30. There is another factor germane to the rise in popularity of football: the media. I'll not explore that here, in part because it has been probed so well and so thoroughly by others. See especially Michael Oriard, *Reading Football: How the Popular Press Created an American Spectacle* (Chapel Hill: University of North Carolina Press, 1995); Oriard, *King Football: Sport & Spectacle in the Golden Age of Radio & Newsreels, Movies & Magazines, the Weekly & the Daily Press* (Chapel Hill: University of North Carolina Press, 2001); Michael Mac-Cambridge, *America's Game: The Epic Story of How Pro Football Captured a Nation* (New York: Random House, 2004).

31. Quoted in Sean Braswell, "Why the U.S. Military Is So Southern," OZY.com, November 20, 2016, https://www.ozy.com/acumen/why-the-us-military-is-so-southern/72100; quoted in Robert B. Mitchell, "Sherman's March to the Sea: A Military Triumph Left a Bitter Legacy," *Washington Post*, September 13, 2014. Ted Ownby writes, "Southern men have always been willing to fight. Feeling a need to assert their wills over any enemy as directly and immediately as possible, and they have used the smallest affront as a reason for combat." Ted Ownby, *Subduing Satan: Religion, Recreation, and Manhood in the Rural South, 1865–1920* (Chapel Hill: University of North Carolina Press, 1990), 12–13.

32. Rick Bragg, "Down Here," ESPN.com, August 8, 2012, https://www.espn.com/college-football/story/_/id/8240383/rick-bragg-explains-history-traditions-south-obsession-football-espn-magazine.

33. Jim L. Sumner, "John Franklin Crowell, Methodism, and the Football Controversy at Trinity College, 1887–1894," *Journal of Sport History* 17, no. 1 (Spring 1990): 5–20.

34. Sumner, "Crowell, Methodism, and the Football Controversy," quotes on 8, 13, 18.

35. Wayne Flynt, *Keeping the Faith: Ordinary People, Extraordinary Lives: A Memoir* (Tuscaloosa: University of Alabama Press, 2011), 124–25; Douglas Stutsman, *The Deep South's Oldest Rivalry: Auburn vs. Georgia* (Charleston, S.C.: History Press, 2017), 33–34. The Georgia team had earlier played, and defeated, Mercer.

36. Stutsman, *Deep South's Oldest Rivalry*, 33–34.

37. Don Wade, *Always Alabama: A History of Crimson Tide Football* (New York: Simon & Schuster, 2006), 4–5; "Greek to Meet Greek: Auburn and Tuskaloosa [*sic*] to Meet in the Arena," *Birmingham Weekly*, January 11, 1893.

38. Eli Gold, *Crimson Nation: The Shaping of the South's Most Dominant Football Team* (Nashville: Rutledge Hill Press, 2005), 25; Wade, *Always Alabama*, 5–7. Van de Graaff's teammates finally prevailed on him to have the ear bandaged.

39. Flynt, *Keeping the Faith*, 124–25; quoted in Patrick B. Miller, "The Manly, the Moral, and the Proficient: College Sport in the New South," *Journal of Sport History* 24, no. 3 (Fall 1997): 285; Eric Bain-Selbo, "From Lost Cause to Third-and-Long: College Football and the Civil Religion of the South," *Journal of Southern Religion*, 11 (2009), http://jsr.fsu.edu/Volume11/Selbo.htm.

40. Quoted in Bragg, "Down Here"; quoted in William J. Baker, *Playing with God: Religion and Modern Sport* (Cambridge, Mass.: Harvard University Press, 2007), 106; quoted in Andrew Doyle, "Turning the Tide: College Football and Southern Progressivism," in *The Sporting World of the Modern South*, ed. Patrick B. Miller (Urbana: University of Illinois Press, 2002), 111; Wade, *Always Alabama*, 9.

41. Baker, *Playing with God*, 106; quoted in Doyle, "Turning the Tide," 110; quoted in Wayne Flynt, *Alabama in the Twentieth Century* (Tuscaloosa: University of Alabama Press, 2006), 419.

42. Scott Eden, *Touchdown Jesus: Faith and Fandom at Notre Dame* (New York: Simon & Schuster, 2005), 144–46.

43. Quoted in Eden, *Touchdown Jesus*, 150.

44. Quoted in Eden, *Touchdown Jesus*, 150, 147, 148.

45. Richard C. Crepeau, *NFL Football: A History of America's New National Pastime* (Urbana: University of Illinois Press, 2014), 24, 6–8.

46. Crepeau, *NFL Football*, 24–25.

47. Crepeau, *NFL Football*, 24–25.

48. Crepeau, *NFL Football*, 25–26; Michael E. Lomax, "The African American Experience in Professional Football," *Journal of Social History* 33, no. 1 (Autumn 1999): 163; quoted in William C. Rhoden, "The N.F.L.'s Embrace

of Black Players Has Always Been Conditional," *New York Times*, December 23, 2019. See also Thomas G. Smith, "Outside the Pale: The Exclusion of Blacks from the National Football League, 1934–1945," in *From Jack Johnson to LeBron James: Sports, Media, and the Color Line*, ed. Chris Lamb (Lincoln: University of Nebraska Press, 2016), 117–47. Regarding Marshall and the integration of the Redskins, see John Florio and Ouisie Shapiro, *One Nation under Baseball: How the 1960s Collided with the National Pastime* (Lincoln: University of Nebraska Press, 2017), 15–16; Ryan Basen, "Fifty Years Ago, Last Outpost of Segregation in N.F.L. Fell," *New York Times*, October 6, 2012. Despite his opposition to integration, Halas nevertheless signed a Jewish player, Sid Luckman, of Columbia University, to the Bears in 1939; Luckman led the team to four NFL championships: 1940, 1941, 1943, and 1946. Kenny Washington has sometimes been described as breaking the color barrier in the NFL, but that ignores the careers of earlier Black players; see Keyshawn Johnson and Bob Glauber, *The Forgotten First: Kenny Washington, Woody Strode, Marion Motley, and the Breaking of the NFL Color Barrier* (New York: Grand Central Publishing, 2021) as an example of this historical revisionism, even though the book contains a passage on Pollard.

49. Charles H. Martin, *Benching Jim Crow: The Rise and Fall of the Color Line in Southern College Sports, 1890–1980* (Urbana: University of Illinois Press, 2010), chap. 1; Patrick B. Miller, "Slouching toward a New Expediency: College Football and the Color Line during the Depression Decade," *American Studies* 40, no. 3 (Fall 1999): 10.

50. Quoted in Miller, "Slouching toward a New Expediency," 16.

51. Quoted in Miller, "Slouching toward a New Expediency," 21.

52. S. Zebulon Baker, "'On the Opposite Side of the Fence': The University of Kentucky and the Racial Desegregation of the Southeastern Conference," *New Directions in Kentucky Sport History* 115, no. 4 (Autumn 2017): 561–610, quote on 602; "Recalling the Death of Racial Segregation in Southern College Football," *Journal of Blacks in Higher Education*, 21 (Autumn 1998), 65; Howard E. Bailey, interview by Gerald L. Smith, October 29, 2011, Greg Page Oral History Project, Louie B. Nunn Center for Oral History, University of Kentucky Libraries. Bailey described Page as "a dear friend who shouldn't have had such a short life."

53. Quoted in Andrew Doyle, "An Atheist in Alabama Is Someone Who Doesn't Believe in Bear Bryant: A Symbol for an Embattled South," in Miller, *Sporting World of the Modern South*, 247–48.

54. Doyle, "Atheist in Alabama," 254–55.

55. Doyle, "Atheist in Alabama," 265; Howell Raines, "Goodbye to the Bear," *New Republic*, January 23, 1983.

56. Doyle, "Atheist in Alabama," 267.

57. Doyle, "Atheist in Alabama," 269–70.

58. Doyle, "Atheist in Alabama," 269–70; David Wharton, "Sam Cunningham, USC Player Who Helped Integrate College Football, Dies at 71," *Los Angeles Times*, September 7, 2021; "Recalling the Death of Racial Segregation," 64–65.

59. Doyle, "Atheist in Alabama," 271.

60. Raines, "Goodbye to the Bear."

61. Andrew Mulligan, "An Ivy League Pioneer," *Dartmouth Alumni Magazine*, September-October 2005, 36–37. I'm grateful to Charles Sherman for alerting me to this incident, and I'm well aware that the "Ivy League" was not formally established until 1954.

62. Lane Demas, *Integrating the Gridiron: Black Civil Rights and American College Football* (New Brunswick, N.J.: Rutgers University Press, 2010), 8–9, chap. 3; "Bright Offensive Leader," *New York Times*, December 11, 1950, 33; "Caught by the Camera," *Life*, November 5, 1951, 121–24. The *Register*'s photographers won the Pulitzer Prize in journalism photography the following year.

63. Wesley Lowery and Jacob Bogage, "Fifty Years after the 'Black 14' Were Banished, Wyoming Football Reckons with the Past," *Washington Post*, November 30, 2019; Demas, *Integrating the Gridiron*, chap. 5.

64. Camp, *Book of Foot-ball*, 93; "Walter Camp," in *First Crusade against Football*, 108; Thwing, "Football a Game of Brains," 43; Dudley A. Sargent, "The Results of Athletics on College Students," *New York Times*, February 4, 1912, 8.

65. "John Langdon Sibley's Diary," in *First Crusade against Football*, 7; "A Last Word," *First Crusade*, 18; "The New York Daily Tribune," *First Crusade*, 48; "The Ackley Independent—Ackley, Iowa," *First Crusade*, 39–40; "The Kennebec Daily Journal—Maine," *First Crusade*, 41.

66. "Ball Contests and Gossip," in *First Crusade against Football*, 43; John M. Murrin, "Rites of Domination: Princeton, the Big Three, and the Rise of Intercollegiate Athletics," paper delivered at Princeton University, October 10, 1996, 31; quoted in Parke Hill Davis, *Football, the American Intercollegiate Game* (New York: Scribner's Sons, 1917), 98; "Yale Again Triumphant," *New York Times*, November 25, 1894.

67. Quoted in Emil R. Salvini, *Hobey Baker: American Legend* (St. Paul, Minn.: Hobey Baker Memorial Foundation, 2005), 33.

68. George E. Merrill, "Is Football Good Sport?," *North American Review*, 177 (November 1903), 759; quoted in John Hammond Moore, "Football's Ugly Decades, 1893–1913," *Smithsonian Journal of History*, 2 (1967): 59; Rowley,

Shared Origins, 193; Ronald A. Smith, ed., *Big-Time Football at Harvard: The Diary of Coach Bill Reid* (Chicago: University of Chicago Press, 1994), 208, 210.

69. Quoted in Michael Beschloss, "T.R.'s Son Inspired Him to Help Rescue Football," *New York Times*, August 1, 2004. See also John J. Miller, *The Big Scrum: How Teddy Roosevelt Saved Football* (New York: Harper, 2011); John S. Watterson III, "Political Football: Theodore Roosevelt, Woodrow Wilson and the Gridiron Reform Movement," *Presidential Studies Quarterly* 25, no. 3 (Summer 1995): 555–64.

70. Charles W. Eliot, "Report of the President of Harvard College, 1893–1894," 16, Harvard College Archives; Rowley, *Shared Origins*, 196–97; Ronald A. Smith, "Harvard and Columbia and a Reconsideration of the 1905–06 Football Crisis," *Journal of Sport History* 8, no. 3 (Winter 1981): 8.

71. Quoted in Beschloss, "T.R.'s Son"; Smith, *Big-Time Football at Harvard*, 194–95.

72. Quoted in Sal Paolantonio, *How Football Explains America* (Chicago: Triumph Books, 2015), 222; Murrin, "Rites of Domination."

73. Jim Morrison, "The Early History of Football's Forward Pass," Smithsonian .com, December 28, 2010, https://www.smithsonianmag.com/history/the -early-history-of-footballs-forward-pass-78015237/; James Surowiecki, "Beautiful. Violent. American. The N.F.L. at 100," *New York Times*, December 23, 2019; Victor Mather and Joe Ward, "From Baugh to Brees, There Is No Slowing the N.F.L. Passing Game," *New York Times*, December 31, 2019. Part of the reason passing increased in the NFL was that the league altered the rules prior to the 1977 season; see Paolantonio, *How Football Explains America*, 206–7.

74. "Intercollegiate Football," in *First Crusade against Football*, 66; Frank Robinson Shipman, *Quarter-Centenary Record of the Class of 1885, Yale University* (Boston: Fort Hill Press, 1913), 280.

CHAPTER 3

1. W. Geo. Beers, *Over the Snow: or, The Montreal Carnival* (Montréal: W. Drysdale, 1881), 15, 11; Leslie McFarlane, "The Wrist Shot," *Sport Story Magazine*, April 10, 1933, 77–86.

2. Allan Downey, *The Creator's Game: Lacrosse, Identity, and Indigenous Nationhood* (Vancouver: UBC Press, 2018), 20. On precursors to hockey, see Frank Cosentino, "Hockey Origins," *Hockey Research Journal*, 18 (2014–15): 61–62.

3. J. Thomas West, "Beers, William George," in *Dictionary of Canadian Biography*, accessed December 3, 2019, http://www.biographi.ca/en/bio/beers _william_george_12E.html.

4. W. G[eorge] Beers, *Lacrosse: The National Game of Canada* (Montréal: Dawson Brothers, 1869), v; Craig Greenham, "Ideological Struggles and the Emergence of Cricket, Lacrosse, and Baseball," in *Sport and Recreation in Canadian History*, ed. Carly Adams (Champaign, Ill.: Human Kinetics, 2021), 125–48, quote on 132.

5. Michael A. Robidoux, "Imagining a Canadian Identity through Sport: An Historical Interpretation of Lacrosse and Hockey," in Jenny Ellison and Jennifer Anderson, eds., *Hockey: Challenging Canada's Game* (Ottawa: Canadian Museum of History and University of Ottawa Press, 2018), 61–75; Beers, *Lacrosse*, 59, 58, xv–xvi. An ethnic essentialist, Beers touted the "rough and ready character" of Anglo-Saxons and puzzled that French Canadians were not "as enthusiastically devoted to out-door sports as their Anglo brethren" (though he admired their love of music).

6. Quoted in Robidoux, "Imagining a Canadian Identity through Sport," 68; Downey, *Creator's Game*, 43.

7. Quoted in Downey, *Creator's Game*, 45, 47, 56 (Downey misquotes the motto on 47).

8. Quoted in Carl Gidén, Patrick Houda, and Jean-Patrice Martel, *On the Origin of Hockey* (Stockholm: Hockey Origin Publishing, 2014), 29.

9. J. W. (Bill) Fitsell, *How Hockey Happened: A Pictorial History of the Origins of Canada's National Winter Game* (Kingston, Ont.: Quarry Press, 2006), 2, 144; Gidén, Houda, and Martel, *On the Origin of Hockey*, 1, 4–5, 20; cf. Iain Fyffe, "Breaking the Ice: How Big-Time Hockey Began in Manitoba," *Hockey Research Journal*, 17 (2013–14): 1–7.

10. Quoted in Fitsell, *How Hockey Happened*, 2; Gidén, Houda, and Martel, *On the Origin of Hockey*, 18–20, quote on 18.

11. Gidén, Houda, and Martel, *On the Origin of Hockey*, 8–14; quoted in Martin Jones, *Hockey's Home: Halifax-Dartmouth: The Origin of Canada's Game* (Halifax, N.S.: Nimbus, 2002), 10–12.

12. Howard Shubert, *Architecture on Ice: A History of the Hockey Arena* (Montreal: McGill-Queen's University Press, 2016), 29, 47–48; John Chi-Kit Wong, *Lords of the Rinks: The Emergence of the National Hockey League, 1875–1936* (Toronto: University of Toronto Press, 2005), 11, 17; Michel Vigneault, "Montreal's Hockey Tradition," *Society for International Hockey Research Journal*, 1 (1993): 8–9. For a brief biographical sketch of Creighton, see Jones, *Hockey's Home*, 85.

13. Fitsell, *How Hockey Happened*, 110; "Hockey in the Victoria Skating Rink," *Montréal Daily Witness*, March 4, 1875; quoted in Gidén, Houda, and Martel, *On the Origin of Hockey*, 23.

14. Fitsell, *How Hockey Happened*, 8, 110, 112, quote on 8.

15. Fitsell, *How Hockey Happened*, 114; quoted in Austin Danforth, "Vermont's Claim to International Hockey History," *Burlington Free Press*, February 26, 2016.

16. J. Andrew Ross, *Joining the Clubs: The Business of the National Hockey League to 1945* (Syracuse, N.Y.: Syracuse University Press, 2015), 19, 18.

17. Victor Russell, "Hockey in Victorian-Era Toronto: The Ontario Hockey Association and the Toronto Bank Hockey League," *Hockey Research Journal*, 20 (2016–17), 2; Barbara Schrodt, "Sabbatarianism and Sport in Canadian Society," *Journal of Sport History* 4, no. 1 (Spring 1977): 30, 23.

18. Russell, "Hockey in Victorian-Era Toronto," 6–7.

19. Russell, "Hockey in Victorian-Era Toronto," 6–7, quote on 7.

20. Russell, "Hockey in Victorian-Era Toronto," 9–11; quoted in Fitsell, *How Hockey Happened*, 124.

21. Quoted in Fitsell, *How Hockey Happened*, 120, 124.

22. Lisa Laughy, "From the Archives: Hockey on Lower School Pond," OhrstromBlog.com, January 26, 2009, http://www.ohrstromblog.com /2009/01/26/from-the-archives-hockey-on-lower-school-pond/.

23. "It All Began with a Handshake: The Hobey Baker Story," Hobey-Baker.com, accessed December 30, 2020, https://www.hobeybaker.com /hobeybakerstory.

24. See Emil R. Salvini, *Hobey Baker: American Legend* (St. Paul, Minn.: Hobey Baker Memorial Foundation, 2005).

25. Ross, *Joining the Clubs*, 20–21; Wong, *Lords of the Rinks*, 15. On the first Stanley Cup, see James Duplacey, "Legends and Facts: The First Presentation of the Stanley Cup," *Hockey Research Journal*, 2 (1994): 13–15.

26. On the fight against professionalism, see Kevin Slater, "Guilty until Proven Innocent: How the Ontario Hockey Association Came to Enact Its Harsh Rules against Professionalism," *Hockey Research Journal*, 21 (2020): 1–6.

27. Ross, *Joining the Clubs*, 29–31.

28. J. W. (Bill) Fitsell, "Doc Gibson: The Eye in the IHL," *Hockey Research Journal*, 8 (Fall 2004): 1–3; Shubert, *Architecture on Ice*, 69–71. On the formation of the International Hockey League, see Daniel S. Mason, "The International Hockey League and the Professionalization of Ice Hockey, 1904–1907," *Journal of Sport History* 25, no. 1 (Spring 1998): 1–17, quote on 5; Bill Sproule, "Houghton: The Birthplace of Professional Hockey," *Hockey Research Journal*, 8 (Fall 2004): 1–4; Ernie Fitzsimmons, "Pittsburgh: The Cradle of Pro Hockey," *Hockey Research Journal*, 13 (Fall 2009): 5–8. It is probably worth noting that both Jack "Doc" Gibson and George Beers were dentists. It may be either coincidence or opportunism—or both! See Bill Sproule, "Hockey and

Dentists: Builders, Players and Stories," *Hockey Research Journal*, 18 (2014–15): 26–31.

29. Ross, *Joining the Clubs*, 35–36; Bill Sproule, "The Allan Cup: Hockey's Second-Oldest Trophy," *Hockey Research Journal*, 14 (Fall 2010): 17–21.

30. Quoted in Ross, *Joining the Clubs*, 45; Wong, *Lords of the Rinks*, 56, 59.

31. Wong, *Lords of the Rinks*, 51–53.

32. Gidén, Houda, and Martel, *On the Origin of Hockey*, 24; Ross, *Joining the Clubs*, 38–40; Michel Vigneault, "The Catholic Connection in Montreal Hockey 1891–1917," *Hockey Research Journal*, 2 (1994): 16–19. On the Canadiens' dominance in the 1970s, see Murray Grieg, "Lords of the Rink: 1976–77 Habs Were the Best Ever," *Hockey Research Journal*, 9 (Fall 2005): 59–60.

33. Wong, *Lords of the Rinks*, 65–68; John Chi-Kit Wong, "Professional Hockey and Urban Development: A Historical Case Study of the Vancouver Arena, 1911–1914," *Urban History Review / Revue histoire urbaine* 38, no. 1 (Fall 2009): 3–14; Shubert, *Architecture on Ice*, 76–78, 80; Eric Zweig, "Setting Cyclone's Record Straight," *Hockey Research Journal*, 11 (Fall 2007): 47–50.

34. Wong, *Lords of the Rinks*, 69. One of the Patricks' recruits to the PCHA was Fred "Cyclone" Taylor; see Len Kotylo, "Cyclone Taylor: The View from the Pacific Coast," *Hockey Research Journal*, 10 (Fall 2006): 16–17.

35. Ross, *Joining the Clubs*, 58–64, quote on 58; Wong, *Lords of the Rinks*, 72–74.

36. On NHL expansion in the 1920s, see Ross, *Joining the Clubs*, chap. 4. See also Stacy L. Lorenz, "'A Lively Interest on the Prairies': Western Canada, Mass Media, and a 'World of Sport,' 1870–1939," *Journal of Sport History* 27, no. 2 (Summer 2000): 195–227. Despite years of informal queries, I have yet to learn why the Toronto Maple Leafs are not the Toronto Maple Leaves; my command of grammar may be faulty, but I was taught that the plural of *leaf* is *leaves*.

37. Quoted in Andrew C. Holman, "A Flag of Tendons: Hockey and Canadian History," in Ellison and Anderson, *Hockey*, 32. For a striking example of "backyard ponds of the frozen north," see Gerald Narcisco, "N.H.L. Draft Pick Inspires Dreams as Big as the Yukon," *New York Times*, January 16, 2020, sect. B, 7.

38. Kevin G. Jones, "Developments in Amateurism and Professionalism in Early 20th Century Canadian Sport," *Journal of Sport History* 2, no. 1 (Spring 1975): 29–40.

39. Bruce Berglund, *The Fastest Game in the World: Hockey and the Globalization of Sports* (Oakland: University of California Press, 2021), 32.

40. Alex Prewitt, "Enter the 'Sin Bin': What It's Like to Be Sent to 'Adult Timeout' in the NHL," *Sports Illustrated*, April 17, 2018. On the influx of

French and Irish Catholics into hockey at the turn of the twentieth century, see Michel Vigneault, "The Catholic Connection in Montreal Hockey 1891–1917," *Society for International Hockey Research Journal*, 2 (1994): 16–19.

41. Quoted in Stanley Kay, "Winter Is Going," *Sports Illustrated*, April 22, 2019, 92. See also John Willis, "In the Beginning Was the Sweater," in Ellison and Anderson, *Hockey*, 85–96.

42. Randy Turner, "Heartbeat of a Small Town: Community Survival Depends on the Vitality of the Local Hockey Rink," *Winnipeg Free Press*, February 19, 2016; interview with Bernie Van De Walle, April 16, 2020; Norm O'Reilly et al., *Ice Hockey in Canada, 2015 Impact Study Summary: The Economic, Social, Community and Sport Benefits of Canada's Favourite Game*, May 13, 2015, https://www.scotiabank.com/ca/common/pdf/Ice-Hockey-in-Canada-Summary-and-Infographic.pdf, quoted in Shubert, *Architecture on Ice*, 11.

43. McFarlane, "Wrist Shot," 77–86; quoted in Turner, "Heartbeat of a Small Town."

44. Quoted in Jack Ludwig, *Hockey Night in Moscow* (Richmond Hill, Ont.: Pocket-Penguin, 1974), 17; Douglas Coupland, *Souvenir of Canada* (Vancouver: Douglas & McIntyre, 2002), 55.

45. Brian Kennedy, "Confronting a Compelling Other: The Summit Series and the Nostalgic (Trans)Formation of Canadian Identity," in *Canada's Game: Hockey and Identity*, ed. Andrew C. Holman (Montreal and Kingston: McGill-Queen's University Press, 2009), 45–62, quote on 52. See also Roy MacSkimming, *Cold War: The Amazing Canada-Soviet Hockey Series of 1972* (Vancouver: Greystone Books, 2012).

46. Interview with Van De Walle, April 16, 2020; quoted in Kennedy, "Confronting a Compelling Other," 58.

47. Dave Zarum, "Hockey Night in Canada," *Canadian Encyclopedia*, accessed January 18, 2020, https://www.thecanadianencyclopedia.ca/en/article/hockey-night-in-canada; cf. Scott Young, *The Boys of Saturday Night: Inside Hockey Night in Canada* (Toronto: McClelland & Stewart, 1991); Michael McKinley, *Hockey Night in Canada* (Toronto: Penguin, 2012).

48. Stephen Marche, "The Meaning of Hockey," *The Walrus*, November 2011, https://thewalrus.ca/the-meaning-of-hockey/.

49. Stephen Smith, "Writing the Twisting History of Indigenous Players," *New York Times*, July 1, 2018, SP4.

50. Smith, "Writing the Twisting History of Indigenous Players"; William Douglas, "A First Nations NHL Player Bypassed by History Is Championed by Dogged Reporter," Color of Hockey.com, May 14, 2018, https://colorofhockey.com/2018/05/14/a-first-nations-nhl-player-bypassed-by-history-is-championed

-by-dogged-reporter/; James Milks, "Was NHL History Made in 1918? The Story of Paul Jacobs," *Hockey Research Journal,* 7 (Fall 2003): 3–4.

51. Neil Davidson, "Former Toronto Leafs Captain George Armstrong Dies," *Toronto Globe and Mail,* January 21, 2021; Richard Goldstein, "George Armstrong, 90, All-Star Who Hoisted 4 Stanley Cups," *New York Times,* January 25, 2021, B7. The ranks of professional hockey almost included another indigenous player, the incomparable Jim Thorpe, who was in negotiations with the Toronto Tecumsehs in 1913, although the two sides never came to terms; Kotylo, "Cyclone Taylor," 26; "Thorpe Was Also a Hockey Player," TomBenjey.com, July 19, 2012, https://tombenjey.com/tag/tecumseh-hockey -club/, accessed February 5, 2021.

52. Smith, "Writing the Twisting History of Indigenous Players."

53. Taylor McKee and Janice Forsyth, "Witnessing Painful Pasts: Understanding Images of Sports at Canadian Indian Residential Schools," *Journal of Sport History* 46, no. 2 (Summer 2019): 175–88.

54. Quoted in Shubert, *Architecture on Ice,* 24.

55. Edward R. Grenda, "The Canadian Game—An Introduction," *Society for International Hockey Research Journal,* 1 (1993): 18; quoted in Berglund, *Fastest Game in the World,* 10.

56. Marche, "Meaning of Hockey."

57. Shubert, *Architecture on Ice,* 21; Grenda, "Canadian Game," 18–19; quoted in Bruce Kidd and John Macfarlane, *The Death of Hockey* (Charlottesville: University of Virginia Press, 1972), 4. On the evolution of hockey equipment, see Glen R. Goodhand, "Is Necessity the Mother of Invention? (The Evolution of Hockey Equipment)," *Hockey Research Journal,* 2 (1994): 9–12. A 2015 study by Pascual Restrepo found that, judging by the number of penalty minutes, NHL players who grew up in Canada's more remote areas— areas typically beyond the reach of law-enforcement authorities—were more violent as players than those from more settled areas. See Pascual Restrepo, "Canada's History of Violence," *New York Times,* October 11, 2015, SR10. Kenneth Colburn Jr. argues that fistfights in hockey are "a social ritual involving respect and honor among players," which constitutes "an informal mode of social control"; see Kenneth Colburn Jr., "Honor, Ritual and Violence in Ice Hockey," *Canadian Journal of Sociology/Cahiers canadiens de sociologie* 10, no. 2 (Spring 1985): 153–70. See also Laura Robinson, *Crossing the Lines: Violence and Sexual Assault in Canada's National Sport* (Toronto: McLelland & Stewart, 1998); Michael D. Smith, "Towards an Explanation of Hockey Violence: A Reference Other Approach," *Canadian Journal of Sociology/Cahiers canadiens de sociologie* 4, no. 2 (Spring 1979): 105–24.

CHAPTER 4

1. Naismith's biographical details are taken from Rob Rains, with Helen Carpenter, *James Naismith: The Man Who Invented Basketball* (Philadelphia: Temple University Press, 2009); and James Naismith, *Basketball: Its Origins and Development*, ed. William J. Baker (Lincoln: University of Nebraska Press, 1996).

2. Quoted in Rains, *James Naismith*, 17.

3. Naismith, *Basketball*, 22; Rains, *James Naismith*, 20.

4. Quoted in Yago Colás, "Our Myth of Creation: The Politics of Narrating Basketball's Origins," *Journal of Sport History* 43, no. 1 (Spring 2016), 43.

5. Naismith, *Basketball*, 23, 27; quoted in Rains, *James Naismith*, 30.

6. Naismith, *Basketball*, 33.

7. Quoted in Rains, *James Naismith*, 34, 35. A children's book also recounts Naismith's invention against the background of this restive class; see John Coy, *Hoop Genius: How a Desperate Teacher and a Rowdy Gym Class Invented Basketball* (Minneapolis: Carolrhoda Books, 2013).

8. Quoted in M. Whitcomb Hess, "The Man Who Invented Basketball," *American Scholar* 18, no. 1 (Winter 1948–1949): 88; Rains, *James Naismith*, 42–43.

9. Naismith, *Basketball*, 46. The rules were transcribed and published in the school newspaper, the *Triangle*, the following month; Naismith, 59.

10. Quoted in Rains, *James Naismith*, 44.

11. Rains, *James Naismith*, 44–46, quote on 45.

12. Naismith, *Basketball*, 163.

13. Naismith, *Basketball*, 163–64, 168. On the origins of the women's game, see Pamela Grundy and Susan Shackelford, *Shattering the Glass: The Remarkable History of Women's Basketball* (New York: New Press, 2005), chap. 1.

14. Naismith, *Basketball*, 169.

15. Rains, *James Naismith*, 56.

16. Rains, *James Naismith*, 155, quoted on 60.

17. Naismith, *Basketball*, 132. On Catholics and basketball, see, for example, Timothy B. Neary, *Crossing Parish Boundaries: Race, Sports, and Catholic Youth in Chicago, 1914–1954* (Chicago: University of Chicago Press, 2016).

18. Quoted in Rains, *James Naismith*, xiv.

19. On the popularity of basketball on reservations, see, for example, Alan Klein, *Lakota Hoops: Life and Basketball on the Pine Ridge Indian Reservation* (New Brunswick, N.J.: Rutgers University Press, 2020).

20. "City Life in the Late 19th Century," Library of Congress, accessed December 27, 2020, https://www.loc.gov/classroom-materials/united-states

-history-primary-source-timeline/rise-of-industrial-america-1876–1900/city
-life-in-late-19th-century/.

21. Quoted in William J. Bouwsma, *John Calvin: A Sixteenth-Century Portrait* (New York: Oxford University Press, 1988), 45, 46.

22. Naismith, *Basketball*, 188.

23. Naismith, *Basketball*, 181–82.

24. Naismith, *Basketball*, 182–83.

25. Naismith, *Basketball*, 62. On basketball as an urban game, see, for example, Pete Axthelm, *The City Game: Basketball from the Garden to the Playgrounds* (Lincoln, Neb.: Bison Books, 1999); Matthew Goodman, *The City Game: Triumph, Scandal, and a Legendary Basketball Team* (New York: Ballantine Books, 2019).

26. Naismith, *Basketball*, 72–73.

27. On the Great Migration, see Isabel Wilkerson, *The Warmth of Other Suns: The Epic Story of America's Great Migration* (New York: Vintage, 2011).

28. "Black History Month: Remembering the YMCA's African-American Pioneers," YMCAChicago.org, February 13, 2018, https://www.ymcachicago.org/blog/entry/black-history-month/.

29. W. Gabriel Selassie, "The Black Fives Basketball and the YMCA," drwgsi.org, February 26, 2015, https://drwgsi.org/the-black-fives-basketball-and-the-ymca/; quoted in Onaje X. O. Woodbine, *Black Gods of the Asphalt: Religion, Hip-Hop, and Street Basketball* (New York: Columbia University Press, 2016), 37.

30. See, for example, Axthelm, *City Game*, 23–25; the names of players are taken from Axthelm's book. On the frustrated attempts to use basketball to vault out of the obscurity of the ghetto, see the documentary *Hoop Dreams*, directed by Steve James, 1994.

31. Axthelm, *City Game*, xv.

32. Woodbine, *Black Gods of the Asphalt*, 64, quotes on 139, 102.

33. Tom Dunkel, *Color Blind: The Forgotten Team That Broke Basketball's Color Line* (New York: Grove Press, 2013), 34–35.

34. Ron Grossman, "How the Harlem Globetrotters Integrated the NBA," *Chicago Tribune*, February 14, 2015.

35. Charles H. Baltimore, "The Negro in Basketball," *Negro History Bulletin*, 15 (December 1951): 50.

36. Quoted in Rains, *James Naismith*, 143.

37. Quoted in Rains, *James Naismith*, 144.

38. Doug Merlino, "Fast Break Basketball: How a Black Coach Revolutionized the Game," BleacherReport.com, April 22, 2011, https://bleacherreport

.com/articles/673434-fast-break-basketball-how-a-black-coach-revolutionized -the-game; quoted in Rains, *James Naismith*, 147.

39. On this game, see Scott Ellsworth, *The Secret Game: A Wartime Story of Courage, Change, and Basketball's Lost Triumph* (New York: Little, Brown, 2015).

40. Quoted in Ellsworth, *Secret Game*, 273.

41. Quoted in Rains, *James Naismith*, 154; on the relationship between Naismith and McLendon, see chap. 11. See also Milton S. Katz, *Breaking Through: John B. McLendon, Basketball Legend and Civil Rights Pioneer* (Fayetteville: University of Arkansas Press, 2010); John B. McLendon and Jacqueline Imani Bryant, "Basketball Coach John B. McLendon: The Noble Revolutionary of U.S. Sport April 5, 1915–October 8, 1999," *Journal of Black Studies* 30, no. 5 (May 2000): 720–34.

42. William Gildea, "I Covered Texas Western's Win Over Kentucky. Here's How I Saw History," *Washington Post*, March 17, 2016; Jesse Washington, "Kentucky Must Reckon with the Full Meaning of Adolph Rupp," theundefeated.com, August 7, 2020, https://theundefeated.com/features/kentucky -must-reckon-with-the-full-meaning-of-adolph-rupp/; Richard Sandomir, "A Game Changed History, but It's Hardly Been Seen Since," *New York Times*, March 28, 2016, D2.

43. Naismith's visit to the 1936 Olympics is covered in Rains, *James Naismith*, chap. 12.

44. Quoted in Naismith, *Basketball*, xv.

45. Quoted in Rains, *James Naismith*, 154, 144.

46. Quoted in Rains, *James Naismith*, 160.

47. Quoted in Rains, *James Naismith*, 169.

CONCLUSION

1. Aaron Spencer, "Seattle-Area Church Cancels Sunday Morning Services for Seahawks-Vikings Game," *Seattle Times*, January 7, 2016, https://www .seattletimes.com/sports/seahawks/bothell-church-cancels-sunday-morning -services-for-seahawks-vikings-game/.

2. Stephen Jay Gould, *Triumph and Tragedy in Mudville: A Lifelong Passion for Baseball* (New York: W. W. Norton, 2003), 24; Miriam Chapin, *Contemporary Canada* (New York: Oxford University Press, 1959), 225–26; William Kilbourn, *Religion in Canada: The Spiritual Development of a Nation* (Toronto: McClelland and Stewart, 1968), 6. See also Tracy J. Trothen, "Hockey: A Divine Sport?—Canada's National Sport in Relation to Embodiment, Community,

and Hope," *Studies in Religion / Sciences Religieuses* 35, no. 2 (2006): 291–305; Eric Bain-Selbo, "Ecstasy, Joy, and Sorrow: The Religious Experience of Southern College Football," *Journal of Religion and Popular Culture* 20, no. 1 (Fall 2008): 1–12; Rebecca T. Alpert, *Religion and Sports: An Introduction and Case Studies* (New York: Columbia University Press, 2015).

3. Michael Lipka, "5 Facts about Religion in Canada," Pew Research Center, July 1, 2019, https://www.pewresearch.org/fact-tank/2019/07/01/5-facts-about-religion-in-canada/; "Religious Landscape Study," Pew Research Center, accessed October 3, 2019, https://www.pewforum.org/religious-landscape-study/; "Measuring Religion in Pew Research Center's American Trends Panel," Pew Research Center, January 14, 2021, https://www.pewforum.org/2021/01/14/measuring-religion-in-pew-research-centers-american-trends-panel/; Derek Thompson, "Three Decades Ago, America Lost Its Religion," *Atlantic*, September 26, 2019.

4. "Sports Radio by the Numbers," *Sports Business Journal*, February 13, 2012, https://www.sportsbusinessdaily.com/Journal/Issues/2012/02/13/In-Depth/Charts.aspx; Alex Ben Block, "Why Sports Radio Is Hitting It out of the Park (analysis)," *Hollywood Reporter*, April 12, 2013, https://www.hollywoodreporter.com/news/why-sports-radio-is-hitting-435666.

5. This paraphrased quotation is from Robert Oden; A. Bartlett Giamatti, *A Free and Ordered Space: The Real World of the University* (New York: W. W. Norton, 1989), 81. This quotation, taken from Giamatti's address to Yale first-year students in 1984, has appeared in different forms; I have quoted it without the phrase inside the em dash: "at least this summer."

6. Regarding Fenway Park, see *Glenn Stout, Fenway 1912: The Birth of a Ballpark, a Championship Season, and Fenway's Remarkable First Year* (Boston: Mariner Books, 2012); Michael Ian Borer, *Faithful to Fenway: Believing in Boston, Baseball, and America's Most Beloved Ballpark* (New York: New York University Press, 2008); quoted in Howard Shubert, *Architecture on Ice: A History of the Hockey Arena* (Montreal: McGill-Queen's University Press, 2016), 95. See also Bob McGee, *The Greatest Ballpark Ever: Ebbets Field and the Story of the Brooklyn Dodgers* (New Brunswick, N.J.: Rutgers University Press, 2005).

7. Shubert, *Architecture on Ice*, 105–7; Robert H. Dennis, "Forever Proud? The Montreal Canadiens Transition from the Forum to the Molson Centre," in *Canada's Game: Hockey and Identity*, ed. Andrew C. Holman (Montreal: McGill-Queen's University Press, 2009), 161–79. For an example of the importance of street processions, see Robert A. Orsi, *The Madonna of 115th Street: Faith and Community in Italian Harlem, 1880–1950*, 3rd ed. (New Haven, Conn.: Yale University Press, 2010).

8. Celeste Freeman, "Dream Team: The Basic Training of America's Ultimate Song Girls," *Los Angeles Times*, September 8, 1991.

9. Thomas Boswell, "Athletes Have the Power to Help America Get It Right, and They're Using It," *Washington Post*, August 28, 2020; Lance Hornby, "National Hockey League, Players Take Bold Steps for Social Justice," *Toronto Sun*, September 3, 2020. On the emergence of the Religious Right, see Randall Balmer, *Bad Faith: Race and the Rise of the Religious Right* (Grand Rapids: Wm. B. Eerdmans, 2021). I'm grateful to Jim Wallis for suggesting this point.

10. Jason Notte, "To Reach Men, Advertisers Dial In to Sports Radio," *New York Times*, August 19, 2018, sect. B, 5. Former Dartmouth football coaches and current NFL assistant coaches Callie Brownson and Jennifer King played in the Women's Football Alliance.

11. "NBA vs WNBA: Revenue, Salaries, Viewership, Attendance and Ratings," WSN.com, July 18, 2019, https://www.wsn.com/nba/nba-vs-wnba/.

12. Robert J. Samuelson, "Great Expectations," *Newsweek*, January 8, 1996, 27; "Women in the Workforce—United States: Quick Take," Catalyst.org, June 5, 2019, https://www.catalyst.org/research/women-in-the-workforce -united-states/; "Women in the Workforce—Canada: Quick Take," Catalyst.com, May 28, 2019, https://www.catalyst.org/research/women-in-the-workforce -canada/.

13. Arlie Russell Hochschild, *Strangers in Their Own Land: Anger and Mourning on the American Right* (New York: New Press, 2016), 202.

14. Quoted in George F. Will, *Men at Work: The Craft of Baseball* (New York: Macmillan, 1990), 173.

15. Quoted in Will, *Men at Work*, 173.

16. Block, "Sports Radio Is Hitting It out of the Park."

17. Roman Ricardo Phillips, "Mudcat Grant," *New York Times Magazine*, December 26, 2021, 29.

18. Quoted in Scott Allen, "The Ballpark Is a Summer Sanctuary. These Fans Help Explain Why They Missed It So Much," *Washington Post*, March 30, 2021.

19. Des Bieler, "Bill Russell Led an NBA Boycott in 1961. Now He's Saluting Others for 'Getting in Good Trouble,'" *Washington Post*, August 27, 2020.

20. Joey Morona, "'Shut Up and Dribble' Laura Ingraham Now Says 'Every American Has the God-Given Right to Speak His Mind on Any Issue,'" Cleveland.com, June 5, 2020, https://www.cleveland.com/entertainment/2020/06 /shut-and-dribble-laura-ingraham-now-says-every-american-has-the-god -given-right-to-speak-his-mind-on-any-issue.html. Ingraham later amended her comments to say that everyone has a right to "speak his mind."

21. Richard Sandomir, "Curt Schilling, ESPN Analyst, Is Fired Over Offensive Social Media Post," *New York Times*, April 20, 2016.

22. Quoted in Hans Urs von Balthasar, *Theo-Drama: Theological Dramatic Theory*, trans. Graham Harrison (San Francisco: Ignatius Press, 1988), 95.

23. Ralph Ellison, *Invisible Man* (New York: Random House, 1952), chap. 1.

24. For an excellent discussion of the ramifications of sports fandom, particularly as it relates to athletes of color, see Erin C. Tarver, *The I in Team: Sports Fandom and the Reproduction of Identity* (Chicago: University of Chicago Press, 2017).

25. Quoted in Joseph L. Price, *Rounding the Bases: Baseball and Religion in America* (Macon, Ga.: Mercer University Press, 2006), 233.

26. Glenn Kessler, Salvador Rizzo, and Meg Kelly, "Trump's False or Misleading Claims Total 30,573 over 4 Years," *Washington Post*, January 24, 2021; David Waldstein, "He Let the Astros Players Slide. Now He's Paying for It," *New York Times*, February 22, 2020. Trump's presidential counselor Kellyanne Conway used the phrase "alternative facts" in an interview on *Meet the Press*, NBC News, January 22, 2017.

INDEX

ABOUT THE AUTHOR

An award-winning historian and Emmy Award nominee, Randall Balmer is the John Phillips Professor in Religion at Dartmouth College, where he also served as inaugural director of the Society of Fellows. After earning the PhD from Princeton University in 1985 and before coming to Dartmouth in 2012, he was Professor of North American Religions at Columbia University for twenty-seven years. He has been a visiting professor at Princeton, Yale, Northwestern, and Emory Universities, and he was visiting professor at Yale Divinity School from 2004 to 2008. He has also taught in the Columbia University Graduate School of Journalism.

He is the author of more than a dozen books, including *Redeemer: The Life of Jimmy Carter* and *God in the White House: How Faith Shaped the Presidency from John F. Kennedy to George W. Bush.* His second book, *Mine Eyes Have Seen the Glory: A Journey into the Evangelical Subculture in America,* now in its fifth edition, was made into a three-part PBS documentary. Dr. Balmer was nominated for an Emmy for writing and hosting that series. His work was anthologized in the ninth edition of the *Norton Reader,* and his commentaries have appeared in newspapers across the country, including the *Los Angeles Times,* the *Des Moines Register,* the *Philadelphia Inquirer,* the *New York Times,* the *Washington Post,* the *Santa Fe New Mexican,* and the *St. Louis Post-Dispatch,* among many others.

Dr. Balmer lives in New Hampshire and New Mexico with his wife, Catharine Randall.